Jonathan I.

TV broadcaster Jonathan Maitland reported for Radio 4's *Today* programme for six years, before moving to BBC 1's *Watchdog*. He currently works for ITV as a reporter on the *Tonight* programme with Trevor McDonald, and has presented two *House of Horrors* series about cowboy builders. *How to Make Your Million from the Internet (And what to do if you don't)* is his first book.

HOW TO MAKE YOUR MILLION FROM THE INTERNET

(AND WHAT TO DO IF YOU DON'T)

THE DIARY OF A SHARE TRADER

Jonathan Maitland

CORONET BOOKS
Hodder & Stoughton

A CIP catalogue record for this title is available from the
British Library

ISBN 0 340 82212 0

Typeset by Palimpsest Book Production Limited,
Polmont, Stirlingshire
Printed and bound in Great Britain by
Mackays of Chatham plc, Chatham, Kent

Hodder and Stoughton
A division of Hodder Headline
338 Euston Road
London NW1 3BH

Acknowledgements

To Kate, who edited this book: thank you for slagging me off at that party or this might never have happened.

To all my friends (especially Mark, possibly the kindest and most tolerant man in the world): thank you for putting up with the Most Boring Man In The World for the last year.

To Mike Lynch: thanks for having two brains but more importantly, A Very Impressive Beard. Grow it back!

Jim McLean, for the appendix.

And for Steve, without whom . . .

Finally, this book is dedicated to the memory of my Mum, who would have enjoyed this whole thing more than anyone.

CONTENTS

PART ONE

Chipping Away at the Surface

Tuesday, 4 January

Today I had an idea. On the train, 45 minutes outside Waterloo International, on the way to Paris. I read an article about something called On-line Trading.

Apparently people are giving up their day jobs to buy and sell stocks and shares over the Internet. This strikes me as a major social phenomenon. It may be what my TV pals call a MUP – a Made-Up Phenomenon – but if the figures are anything to go by, I doubt it: 50,000 people are doing it already, and every week 3,000 new people are logging on for the first time. There seems to be a mass outbreak of DIY stockbroking going on. And lots of people are, apparently, making lots of money out of it.

Normally, this wouldn't interest me, for three reasons:

1) I am a complete and utter E imbecile. I haven't even exposed myself to the Net's rays, let alone surfed its waves.

2) My knowledge of stocks and shares could fit safely up a gnat's arse.

3) I've never been interested in making money as an end in itself.

But the thing is, my mate Richard does it. I love Richard. I have known him for 25 years, ever since he won my friendship by luring me round to his mum's for a piece of chocolate cake. Richard is safe. He is normal. He has been in the same mood for the last 25 years: calm, unflappable, nonplussed. He doesn't take risks. He has worked for the family firm, which refurbishes pubs, all his life. He lives in Norbiton, which is even more boring than Surbiton.

And he is trading stocks and shares on the Internet. He started last month. If Richard is doing it, Something Really Must Be Happening Out There. My idea, then: as a purely journalistic exercise, I will mortgage my house for £50,000. I will try and turn it into a million, by the end of this year, buying and selling stocks and shares via the Internet. And I will keep a diary of my progress. Everyone else out there seems to be making money, so why can't I? What have I got to lose?*

I will sleep on it and make a final decision tomorrow.

Wednesday, 5 January

Oh, God. Why not? I'm single. I have no dependants. Tomorrow I will go to the Woolwich at Clapham Junction and Do It.

Friday, 7 January

Things are moving quickly. At the Woolwich I met a clean-cut bloke called Sebastian who asked me what the £50,000 was for.

For a moment I contemplated pretending it was for an attic extension, just in case he refused to help. But instead he smiled, said 'Really?', and seemed to think it was all jolly good fun. I am getting a fast-track mortgage deal, which means the cash should be in my account within four weeks.

My other problem is that I don't have a computer. However: Sally, Attractive Blonde American Divorced Mother Of Two from number 25, says she will help me buy one. She also told me she used to be a broker on Wall Street in the 80s. Previously our relationship has consisted largely of me coming round to borrow cans of tuna and watch cricket on Sky. I think I will be seeing a lot more of her in the months to come.

Saturday, 8 January

Spent the morning with Sally (ABADMOT) from No. 25. I couldn't be arsed to wade through three million different computer options so I gave her my credit card and told her to do her worst. Within four minutes she had spent £1,400 of my money and ordered me something from Gateway (I thought they

---

*My house.

sold sausages) complete with mysterious-sounding features like 'mini tower case front panel', 'scanner' and 'emergency start-up diskette'. She was smiling a lot and promised she'd put it together when it arrived.

Sunday, 9 January
Bumped into Velda from Number 43. She refused to buy my four-year-old Canon word processor at the knock-down price of £50. I'm not too bothered about junking it as I've never quite learned to use it properly anyway. I bought it so I could plonk out the lyrics to Burt Bacharach songs for Jackie, the singer in my band, Surf 'n' Turf, but on more than one occasion I've unaccountably made a whole batch of them disappear and had to start all over again. Mind you, it is impressively chunky and as such would make a magnificent doorstop.

Intriguingly, when I told Velda what I was doing, she told me she was doing it already. Fuck me, I said, our road is turning into a mini Wall Street.

'I know. It's very exciting. Oxford Biomedics is a good one, you should try that apparently. Affinity, they're good, my friend Tony bought five hundred pounds of them three months ago, they're now worth six thousand . . .'

It all seems rather straightforward to me. You just pick your companies, sit back and get rich. No wonder everyone's at it.

Monday, 10 January
It can't be that easy. Surely?

Tuesday, 11 January
Today I realised what is making me do this. It's not just money: I'm not that motivated by it. It's more to do with obsession, and what it can achieve.

Let me explain. At various times in my life I have been obsessed with 1) music, 2) golf, 3) cricket, 4) having a good time and 5) being on the telly.

I have no natural ability whatsoever at any of these, apart from number 4, and yet I have achieved a satisfactory level of minimum competence at all of them, through application and not much else.

In 1994, for instance, I got so into golf I kept detailed records of every round I played that year (116, plus 12 holes on a course in Wiltshire before it got too dark). Tragically I reached a glass ceiling very early (a handicap of 24: relatively shit, but not completely useless).

Likewise music. One day, aged 36, I decided I wanted to take my love of pop music further, by being in a band. Looking back, the whole thing bears the hallmarks of the first rumblings of a mid-life crisis, but at the time all I could think of was playing Burt Bacharach songs to people in Italian bistros as they ate. I chose bass on the basis that it only had four strings, and as such had to be easier than the guitar (six).

I got obsessed straight away: within days I was ringing up friends and playing crap bass riffs down the phone to them. But then, as with golf, my head hit the glass ceiling depressingly early. As a result most Tamla Motown songs are well beyond my reach, which distresses me greatly. But even so I've found three friends to play with me in Surf 'n' Turf (our motto: 'Proper music played by professionals'), mainly, I suspect, because I am 'The Man With The Van' – i.e. the bloke you find in every band who is dangerously lacking in musicianship, but cannily has made himself indispensable in other ways, such as transport, equipment and finding gigs.

Determination alone has got me this far (e.g. 'Black Magic Woman' by Santana but not 'I Want You Back' by the Jackson 5). But I will never be a good musician as I have no natural talent.

What fascinates me about the stock market is whether you need talent at all: will sheer determination, on its own, suffice?

If so, I could be quids in. If I get as addicted to making money as I have been to golf, music, etc., will I be able to coin it?

I'm also tired of reading about all those little squirts straight out of university who are supposedly worth £23 million. How come they are, and I'm not? Surely I, a reasonably intelligent journalist, can get himself a piece of the action too? Something Is Happening Out There And I Want To Be Part Of It.

I reckon on-line trading could turn into The New Gambling.

For a start, it's cleaner than going into betting shops – which are dirty, sleazy, and full of drunk bozos smoking roll-ups.

It's also less risky: if you put £50 on a horse and it loses, tough: you've lost the lot. But put £50 on a share, and even if it's a dud you still get a second chance. Something Is Definitely Happening Out There And I Want To Be A Part Of It.

Wednesday, 12 January
Things are happening fast. The computer got delivered this morning. Or rather six huge cardboard boxes containing various bits of it did. Sally put it together in under two hours. And before I knew it I was surfing the World Wide Web. Or rather she was, on my behalf.

In her capacity as my cyberchauffeur she also got me signed up with an on-line share trading company. I am now ready to shoot.

The trouble is my loan isn't due for at least another two and a half weeks. In the meantime I will start anyway: tomorrow I'll play with a few hundred quid of my own, just to get a feel of things, so that when the 50k comes, I'll be able to hit the ground running.

Thursday, 13 January
Hang fire: have been called up to Granada HQ in Manchester to record my commentary for a report on the NHS. Got chatting

to Uncle Trevor (McDonald). He is a rarity: a grade-A celebrity TV presenter who is friendly and decent. An awful lot of them are socially unacceptable (all right, then, wankers) and the question that's been bugging me for years is: why?

But first: an example. Here's a story about a grade-A TV presenter who's been at the top of his profession for more than two decades.

We'll call him Martin.

Martin was interviewing a Top Hollywood Star: it all went well and afterwards the Star very generously invited Martin and the camera crew to stay for a drink on his verandah overlooking the sea. The crew loved it: here they were, relaxing in the sunshine, being served drinks by one of the most famous actors in the world. But Martin was edgy. He was used to being the centre of attention. And he wasn't. The Star's assistant, sensing Martin's unease, tried to make conversation. 'We had xxxxx here last week, he was a very nice man – very successful too. Why don't you have him on your show?'

Martin's face clouded over. 'What the *fuck* would I want him on my show for? It's not that fucking kind of show, for God's sakes! Christ!'

And with that, Martin picked up his jacket and stormed off back to his hotel.

The Hollywood Star was dumbfounded: everyone went quiet.

Thankfully, one of the researchers, who'd seen Martin do this before, quickly sat down next to the Hollywood Star and politely steered the conversation and the atmosphere back into calmer waters.

Martin is by no mean an exception: so to return to my question, why do so many two-bit TV celebs act like this? And how come they get away with it?

I think it's because they've become pathologically accustomed to being fawned over: as a result they have forgotten the rules of normal social interaction. They're fawned over, constantly, because the success of their TV programme relies, to a certain extent, on them being happy. If they are, they give a good performance on-screen; if they're not, they won't, and the show will suffer. Also, anyone who talks to the TV celeb like a normal human being – by telling him or her that they're doing something wrong, for example – is liable to be fired, as the TV celeb has a lot of power. So this makes everyone doubly fawning. End result: star gets away with socially unacceptable behaviour and soon, before you know it, has turned into a fully fledged monster.

Uncle Trevor, I am pleased to say, is not like that at all. He chomps cigars, talks about cricket a lot, loves poetry, and is nice to everyone. And guess what. Even he is sniffing. He too is thinking of buying and selling stocks and shares on the Internet.

Friday, 14 January

Have a slight case of mañana syndrome. Will start next week. Apparently the City Slickers column in the *Daily Mirror* is very good: it gives share tips in a racy, simple-to-understand style and they are constantly crowing about how much money they make for their readers. Sounds promising. Will investigate.

Monday, 17 January

08.00: Am ready to start trading. I have earmarked a company which I am confident will go like a rocket during the course of the day. I will put £200 on it now, sell at the end of the day, and swagger off with a hefty profit.

10.00: No I won't. Spent 46 minutes trying to locate the right bit of the Internet. I.E. got lost on the ruddy 'cyber high street' that everyone's always banging on about. Tried the helpline: spent 28 minutes on hold. Then spent further 14 minutes talking to a bloke called Hugh who tried to guide me in. After seven unsuccessful attempts to 'log on', gave up to go to work.

Tuesday, 18 January

08.30: Yesterday I spent one and a half hours lost in the the cyberforest, unsuccessfully searching for the gateway that would say 'Enter here to start trading stocks and shares on-line'. This morning I found that gateway after just 30 seconds: a brief stroll and there it was, inviting me in.

It happened dead quick. I logged on to the 'dealing site' of the share trading company I registered with last week, and there was a question. 'What share do you want to buy?' I typed the name of the company I fancied – Viglen – into the box, and within two seconds a panel flashed up in front of me, asking how much I wanted to spend. I clicked out '200 pounds'. Immediately, a ruddy great message appeared in the top left-hand corner of my screen. 'You have 15 seconds left to execute the deal.' What? The numbers started changing: '14, 13, 12, 11 . . .' It was a countdown! Blimey. Talk about makeyour-minduptime. I needed longer.

I went back to the lounge, prostrated myself on the sofa with the *Daily Mirror* and reread the City Slickers column. It was written, as always, by two young blokes, Anil Bhoyrul and James Hipwell. Their picture was at the top of the page: they looked a bit spivvy. But I liked what they wrote: it was racy and readable. After tipping a share they would say things like 'Fill your boots on this one'. Or 'Plenty of pie and mash to be had here'.

What they'd written about Viglen seemed to me to make pretty good sense. Under the headline 'SUGAR TO JOIN NET GOLDRUSH: VIGLEN WEB SPIN-OFF WILL SEND SHARES SOARING' they broke the news that a) Alan Sugar's company was starting a separate Internet division, b) the current share price of 180p was 'the bargain of the century' and c) the announcement would 'send the shares soaring to well over 270p today'.

I did some rough sums, quickly. If I bought £300 worth at

180p and they indeed went to 270p today, and I sold them at that point, I'd make £150 profit. Just like that. At the press of a button. Real money: 80 onion bhajees, 5 bottles of champagne. The entire Sheryl Crow CD collection.

I went back to the screen and typed in the letters. V-I-G-L-E-N. The price was now 260p. The shares did indeed appear to be 'soaring'. What the fuck. Let's go! I typed £300 into the box, clicked, and one second later got a message saying a) that I'd bought the shares and b) that I'd been charged £11.99 for the privilege. It felt strange. I'd just carried out a sizable financial transaction and yet no money had changed hands – I hadn't quoted a credit card number, nothing. Just a click of a button, and I was £300 poorer. Thank God I hadn't double-clicked. (I've been reading horror stories about people accidentally buying several thousand pounds' worth of shares twice owing to Over-Active Finger Syndrome.)

It felt seductive. Dangerously seductive. Feeling pleased with myself, I went to work.

13.00: Checked the share price before going to lunch – 340p. Blimey!

14.00: Checked it again – 355p. That means I've made approximately £10 in the time it's taken me to eat a smoked chicken and avocado salad at the pricey Galleria Charlick, the sandwich-bar-cum-picture-gallery on Gray's Inn Road, just a ciabatta roll's throw away from the ITN building, where I work. Even if you take into account the cost of the salad – £4.25 – I was earning almost one pound in pure profit every ten minutes of my lunch break. Greed is good, ladies and gentlemen. It tastes even better than a smoked chicken and avocado salad. I am going to buy some red braces.

16.15: Raced back home and got the computer running. Logged on – 360p!!!! I am going to sell.

16.20: Sold. I've made more than £100 today. This is great!

Wednesday, 19 January

There's a line from a song – I dunno which one – 'we become what we despise'. I used to hate people who played golf. Then I became one.

I used to hate city types who read the *Financial Times*. In the last two weeks I've bought it every day. At first it was like reading a rocket science manual printed in Greek, but now I'm slowly beginning to unlock some of the mysteries of that weird language investors use. A share price that has a 'substantial downside' is one for which the outlook is bleak, i.e. you can lose a lot of money on it. And I'm picking up the sayings. Sally ABADMOT keeps quoting one that worries me. 'When Main Street Talks Wall Street Walks', i.e. when the great unwashed like me, who supposedly know bollock-all about investing, start swapping share tips, then the professionals know it's time to walk away and cash in their chips, coz there's a crash coming. I have read 42 articles about this and they all go on about the way the bubble burst in the late 80s and people were throwing themselves out of tall buildings. Then there's the oft-quoted Dutch tulip craze of the early 17th century, when, at one point in the madness, a single Dutch tulip bulb could be sold for the price of a large house in Mayfair. But this phenomenon, it seems to me, is different: it's based on what many are calling a genuine industrial revolution – the Internet – which is sweeping away the need for expensive things like buildings, and staff. I hope I'm right, anyway.

That is why I am on my way to Mr Samad, who runs the Worst Little Corner Shop In The Universe Let Alone London SW11, to buy today's *FT*.

I don't go to Samad's out of choice; it has been thrust upon me.

Last year I fell out with his rival, the supremely well-stocked Mr Bedi, over some loose change. He shouted at me in front of customers and I threatened to boycott him unless he apologised. He didn't and told me to get out. The wounds still run deep.

Unfortunately, owing to my highly principled stand, I am in a similar position to Cuba, owing to their inability to trade with America: my fridge is regularly bare. This is due to Mr Samad's superhumanly useless approach to running a 'convenience store'. The place looks like the *Marie Celeste*: yesterday, as always, there were vast expanses of empty (and dirty) shelf, populated only by the odd lonely-looking can of baked beans or tuna. He did have two boxfuls of Xmas glitter spray, though (very canny in the middle of January).

He hasn't quite, it seems to me, grasped the basic laws of running a shop: i.e. get the stock in *before* the customer demands it. Whenever I ask for a basic item he holds his head in his hands and says, 'Oh dear. I get wife to cash and carry tomorrow.' And today, guess what. He's run out of copies of the *FT*.

Today, though, for once, I guess it's not really his fault. It's a sign of the times. SW11 has turned into Wall Street: everyone is At It. Distressingly, though, from where I'm standing, I can see Bedi's news-stand. And it's overflowing with pink. I haven't broken my trade embargo for eight months. Should I do it now? That would mean an end to my satisfyingly regular protest/taunting ritual, which involves me walking past his shop window, ignoring him, holding a wrinkled carrier bag of whatever meagre goods I've bought from Samad's triumphantly aloft.

('Look how much trade you're missing out on, pal').

I cannot lose face now. I will get Michael from the dry cleaner's to go in undercover for me.

Oh dear. Michael has fallen out with him and is boycotting him too.

Hold on . . . Bedi is walking away from his shop, leaving his quiet, pacifist wife behind the counter.

I take a deep breath. I run up to the stall, grab an *FT*, burst into the shop, leave a quid on the counter, shout 'Keep the change' and run out again, all before a startled Mrs Bedi has time to speak. Mission accomplished.

Wednesday, 26 January

This isn't going to be quite as easy as I thought. In the last week I have 'day traded' every day, i.e. bought shares in the morning and sold them several hours later. The trouble is, taking into account the dealing charge (£12 each time I buy, £12 each time I sell), I have made a loss on roughly 50% of my trades. On another 20% of the companies, I made a loss even *before* making allowances for the dealing charges: the share prices actually fell during the day, and I had to sell at a loss. I waved goodbye to my £100 Viglen profit a long time ago: I am now £350 down. I am a mug.

This is how things look at the moment (I thought this would be more appropriate than a share graph):

Roof tiles (350 quid's worth) falling off, following disastrous day trading experiment

Last night I had a Day Trader's Dark Night Of The Soul: at this rate my 50k will be worth fuck-all by the end of the year. I need to do something about it, and fast. Someone told me about a bloke who was named the *Sunday Times* 'Fantasy Fund Manager Of The Year' in 1994 and suggested I ask him for advice.

(The competition involved investing a million pounds' worth of notional money: he was the runaway winner.) Apparently he was Asian, called Manek, and ran a chemist's shop in Essex. I have tracked him down, and just now I rang him. He seems to have moved on a bit. A woman answered the phone.

'Hello, Manek Investments here. Can I help you?'

Thursday, 27 January

20.00: I think I have just had the share trader's equivalent of a Road To Damascus conversion. I spent an hour with Jayesh Manek, in his office (it was above his chemist's shop, in Ruislip High Street), and now I know what's meant by the saying 'Every market has its fool and if you don't know who it is, it's probably you'. I never stood a chance.

As Jayesh explained, if you follow a share tip that day just because it's in the paper, you're bound to get shafted a lot of the time: the people in the stock market who set the prices will have read that paper before you, and raised the price accordingly, before trading starts. That way they make money out of all the mugs and lemmings like me who wade into it first thing.

The mugs and lemmings think the share tippers are great because they've correctly identified a share whose price has risen, but often it's just a self-fulfilling prophecy: it's gone up *because* it's been tipped. The key, he said, is to forget trading every day. You need to take a long-term view, and work out which look like good bets in the months/years ahead. Select ten: bung money in each of them, and sit back. Even if only three or four come good, their gains should outweigh the losses.

Some of the tips in the papers are good ones, he said, but they're not going to blossom in a day.

Day traders, I now realise, are kept in the dark, and fed a mixture of shit and bread; but because it's so dark, they can't tell which is which.

People like Jayesh, on the other hand, eat bread and not much else: ten minutes into our chat a woman walked in and asked him to sign a cheque for £10,000.

He was unfailingly polite and sweet, although he probably doesn't throw very good parties. The only time he became slightly animated was when he started drawing me share graphs on scraps of paper. When I asked him what he did in his spare time, he said, 'I read about investments. It is really fascinating. I invest money for 22,000 people, many of them from Ruislip. I have turned £50 million into £200 million in four years. I can never know enough.'

I know enough to know that I know nothing.

In fact, the more I know, the more I know the less I know.

Monday, 31 January

I have been burying my head in the financial pages of all the newspapers, staring at sentences until I understand them. With some articles I've given up, but I am at least getting a bit of a feel for the subject. And talking to everyone who knows anything about the city. And of course the myriad who don't.

There was an interesting article in the *FT* today about a bloke with a beard called Mike Lynch. He runs a company called Autonomy, in Cambridge. It makes software for computers. Apparently the design for it was based on a mathematical equation that had been devised by a bishop in the 18th century, to prove the existence of God.

He – Mike Lynch, not God – was pictured kneeling beside his dog. He also had a beard. Mike Lynch that is, not the dog.

From what I can make out, Mike Lynch seems to have been able to make computers, in effect, understand human language.

He hasn't enabled them to recognize strings of words and act on them, which is what they already do, he has actually given them the ability to ascertain meaning.

That means, if I'm right, he's made a small, but highly significant step, on the path towards imbuing computers with human characteristics. And that, it seems to me, is a big leap.

And even if ultimately he doesn't succeed, or even if I've got it all hopelessly wrong, who cares? It's a bloody good story anyway.

Crucially, he also has a beard. My mate Timo says this is always the first thing he looks for when investing in a company.

His argument is that a chief executive with a beard is much less likely to be in the papers, as he's not nearly as photogenic as someone without a beard, ie Martha Lane Fox. Therefore his company won't get massive hype, à la Lastminute.com, and so won't be in danger of being massively and fatally overvalued. If you are a CEO with a beard, he reckons, you look more bookish, more believable: which is always useful when you're persuading big city types who control mega pension funds to invest several million in you.

I had a close look at the photo. Mike Lynch had a most impressive beard. Thick and lustrous, but not bushy. With a nice matt-black finish.

I discussed all this with Sally at her place tonight . . . I went over for a cup of tea and ended staying for dinner. She is an attractive woman but I don't really fancy her: I like her as a friend. I don't think she fancies me either, so that's fine.

PS: Opponents of Beard Investment Theory will of course quote the obvious example of Richard Branson. He has a beard, they will argue, and yet he gets loads of publicity. To them I say this: he doesn't count. His facial hair is a bit wispy and blond, and therefore doesn't qualify as a proper beard. Beards, for the purposes of Beard Investment Theory, should be thick and dark.

PART TWO
Digging Deeper

Tuesday, 1 February

I have been looking at other companies. One is Marks and Spencer. As I am learning, when you put dosh into a company it helps if you a) know what it does and b) feel comfortable about it. Marks and Spencer scores big time on both these counts.

I was raised on their trifles: my mother, a small, irrational Jewish woman, had a season ticket at M and S. Our fridge (friends called it 'the Tardis' because it looked small on the outside but massive once you opened it) should have had the company logo emblazoned on its door.

I can remember its daily contents even now: M and S sausages on the bottom shelf (cooked, stacked up high on a plate), M and S chicken liver pâté and tubs of M and S coleslaw on the next one up, and M and S bread and M and S tandoori chicken on the top. And M and S fruit trifles bloody everywhere. I reckon they must have put drugs in those things, which made you not want to stop eating them: before I knew what was happening I was putting away a family-sized trifle every day. Which is why I weighed 15 stone by the time I was 14. Anyway, the food at M and S is still the business, although these days I go there for stir-fry veg, fruit salad and skinless chicken breasts. Times have changed.

The way I see it, their products are still good, people will always buy them, so why not invest? Another plus is that the share price is dead low – around 230p, half of what it was a year ago. The only way is up, it seems to me.

Also, because their share price is low, it wouldn't cost much to buy the entire company: at least not nearly as much as when the share price was high. This means they are an attractive proposition for big predators who know a bargain when they see one. If that happens, i.e. there's a takeover bid, the share price will go up.

One to think about.

* * *

I have been finding out more about Autonomy. Apparently one of the most important things you should look for in a company when you're thinking of putting big dosh into them is whether the 'barriers to entry' are high. High = Good. Low = Bad.

Basically, if Your Chosen Company Ltd (YCC) is engaged in an activity where the barriers to entry are high, it will be difficult for other companies to emulate what YCC are doing. Which means YCC then has an effective monopoly in its chosen market and a bit of a licence to print money. On the other hand, if any old sod can do what they're doing, i.e. the barriers to entry are low, then things are going to be a bit tougher. So, big question. What is the state of Mike Lynch's barriers? Solid, methinks. Autonomy has developed software which has had every word of every language in the world fed into it. Yes, every word of every language in the world (including two versions of Mandarin . . . attention to detail or what!). A different mathematical symbol has then been assigned to every word, which means the computer can differentiate between those words, recognise them, and, crucially, understand them. This means, for instance, that if you send an e-mail in English to someone in France, Autonomy will ensure that the recipient's version is in French. Neat!

Even more useful (and potentially lucrative) is the fact that Autonomy can sift through and filter the billions of gallons of crap that are out there on the Internet, and make sense of it all. This, I think, could be a big deal: at the moment the big problem with the World Wide Web is that it's a bit like the British Library after a hurricane has hit it, i.e. all the books are in a pile on the floor and if you want to find something out, you haven't a clue where to start.

Yes, I know there are search engines, but in my limited time in cyberspace I have already experienced their limitations: type in 'T. Rex' and you could get 4,000 sites to choose from, including not just ones on the (completely fantastic) 70s band, but also the prehistoric animal, and the supermarket pastry.

Autonomy, however, will have divined from your previous computer use that you are a bit of a T. Rex fan, and so will bring you only stuff on the band and nothing else.

So if you run a pension fund, for example, and you hold billions of shares in Mongolian pig futures, and there's a mass outbreak of beriberi among Mongolian pigs, which means they're all going to die, Autonomy will ensure that you get to hear about it pretty quick: in fact it can even come to your screen, of its own accord, seconds after it's appeared in data anywhere on the World Wide Web. You will then have a huge advantage, as you will be able to sell your shares before anyone else.

This is what I call a bit of a head start. A head start, I presume a lot of people would pay a lot of money for.

So, back to the big question. How difficult is Autonomy to emulate?

Well, put it this way: I don't know too many people who've spent the last few years feeding every word of every single language in the world into a computer.

On the other hand, any old arse, it seems to me, can do what Lastminute.com do (i.e. sell cut-price holidays, meals, and so on). In fact a lot of people already are: and arguably, doing it better.

So: those barriers. I reckon Lynchy's would do justice to a tungsten-gated medieval castle surrounded by a moat filled with boiling oil.

Lastminute's look as forbidding as a country stile.

Lynchy himself has an interesting analogy, which keeps getting quoted in the press. He says the only people who made a fortune in the Gold Rush were the ones who supplied picks and shovels to the mob who went looking for it. Autonomy, he claims, are doing the cyber equivalent.

In which case, outfits like Lastminute.com are among the

thousands of high-street jewellers selling the rings made out of that gold. Even more worryingly for Martha and Co., what happens if (when?) one of Lastminute's main customers, like British Airways, realise that they can make more selling their flights *themselves* over the Internet, rather than letting Lastminute do it for them?

I know what I've just written sounds like an advert, but I can't help it: I'm trying to be sceptical, but I'm failing. With Lastminute, though (and the rest), it's hard not to be.

I know where I'm putting my money.

In fact, I think I know where I'm putting an awful lot of my money.

Wednesday, 2 February

My flirtation with Marks and Spencer is over. Mainly because of a chat I had with the extremely wholesome and not unattractive Katie Derham, the ITN newscaster, at work today. As part of my essential background research I enquired whether she would be prepared to wear, daily, nothing but M and S outfits while reading the news. If the answer was yes, I figured, M and S would be a good bet: the story would eventually get in the papers ('Lovely TV Katie wears M and S') and so hordes of Katie wannabes would then besiege M and S stores buying up everything in sight. This, in turn, would lead to a pleasing hike in the share price. Alas, Katie said words to the effect that she wouldn't be seen dead on TV in M and S. Although she did favour their underwear. In fact, she said, she was wearing some right now. This last bit sent a mild frisson through me, but not enough to open my wallet and buy a chunk of the company. In fact a straw poll of the rest of the women in the *Tonight* office revealed much the same thing.

Investing in the stock market at present is, I think, a bit like sex: you should aim for explosive growth, as quickly as possible,

and then pull out at the right moment. The M and S ladies'
underwear market might give me growth — in fact, if I was
running the company right now I would be getting into women's
knickers in a big way, so to speak — but it will not give me *explosive* growth.

Which begs the question: why not? Well, as far as I can tell,
it's all to do with profit margins. M and S's are small. One of
their (admittedly rather tasty) ready-made lasagnes, for instance,
might cost you three quid, but for M and S the pure profit
element of that might be, say, around 20p.

Which isn't huge. This is because of all the things they have
to pay for on the way . . . the product itself, of course, the wages
of the people who make it and package it, and so on.

Then there's the cost of distributing it: and of maintaining and
staffing their huge and extremely expensively located high-street
stores. What are the prospects for explosive growth there? Unless
they can suddenly find a way of making and delivering and selling
the lasagne for 3p, not much. There may well be steady growth,
mind you, but not explosive. And if I'm going to make a million
by the end of the year I need explosive growth.

High-technology companies, on the other hand, do offer the
potential of explosive growth. (Note use of the word 'potential'
here.) They have no high-street buildings to look after, employ
relatively small numbers of staff, and have pretty low product
costs.

This is because, often, their main product is, essentially, information. (Cost: nothing.) Which brings me back to Autonomy. Their
profit margins are staggeringly high. For every £100 of software
they sell, £93 is pure profit. They are also operating in an industry
('Knowledge Management') which is growing at a rate of 250%
a year.

And — this is the key part, so pay attention — experts (i.e.
analysts) reckon Autonomy's slice of the market could be,

eventually, worth as much as *fifteen billion quid*. At the moment, given the company is worth around two billion, there is plenty of room for growth.

That's the theory, anyway. The trouble is, things are happening so fast in cyberland, it could all go wrong. Somebody might find that the analysts have miscalculated, or have been over-optimistic. Or – horror of horrors – an American Mike Lynch might suddenly emerge from Silicon Valley, with a bigger and more lustrous beard, and software that does everything that Mike's does, and more. In which case Autonomy will find they have a warehouse full of the cyberspace equivalent of typewriters on their hands.

But – looking on the bright side – Autonomy are at least making profits. Real, cash ones. A lot of the other hi-tech and Internet companies around at the moment are so new, they're not anywhere *near* Profitsville. Yet. So, when people buy into them they are doing so on the basis of fabulous amounts of wonga pouring into company coffers at some unspecified date in the future. It's all about confidence, you see.

The trouble is, if something makes that confidence go . . . it could turn ugly. Let's just say, for example, that a group of key investors suddenly decide that they can't wait for those fabulous future profits any longer. They desert the hi-tech companies in droves. Sentiment – the most valuable (or damning) commodity there is – then starts to turn. Whispers in the City will turn to roars: Internet prophets will turn into pariahs overnight. Hi-tech share prices will fall, quickly. The problem for you and me is that it will be smaller investors who get their fingers singed/burned to a stump. Because it will often be the smaller investor who's last to cotton on that it's time to sell. By which time the City Big Boys will be on their way to Rio, in First Class, with smiles on their faces and nary a twinge on their consciences.

It's called capitalism.

The reason the Big Boys – the banks and institutions – have

that advantage is because they get the information first and, crucially, they (usually) know what to do with it. The nightmare scenario is that by the time they've finished selling, there may be nothing much left for the likes of you and me to sell anyway.

The moral here, as I'm finding out, is that successful investing is largely a question of reading the psychology of the market correctly. Is it confident (i.e. 'a bull market')? And, more importantly, how long will it remain so?

At the moment, any old twat can tell that hi-tech shares aren't just bullish, they've got mad cow tendencies. But working out when the bull is likely to drop dead from exhaustion is far more difficult.

Equally worrying is the prospect of the buying and selling system getting overloaded, and breaking down, just at the crucial moment. There are signs of this happening already, in fact: there was a story in the papers the other day about a bloke who'd been put on hold while waiting to speak to his broker. He (the customer) wanted to sell, but was kept waiting for ages. During that time the price of his shares plummeted. He ended up losing £9,000 in 35 minutes.

He got off lightly: someone else reportedly suffered a heart attack while on hold.

The big question is: what starts a crash? What makes investors lose confidence? Well, it could be anything. It could be new research, showing that people aren't, in fact, going to use the Internet in order to buy the entire contents of their fridge/ wardrobe/bookshelves/whatever. Or a study which shows that sitting in front of your PC damages your health. Or a pronouncement from A Very Well-Respected Big Cheese In The Financial World, saying something like. 'This Internet share price thing is all bollocks and it's got to stop.'

That's not happening at the moment, but if it does, it's Crash

City. I hope it won't happen, however, as I am going for hi-tech companies in a big way. Well, one in particular.

I am bunging £30,000 on the Autonomy Beard Corporation. Am I being stupid? I hope not. I don't think so. Do I feel nervous?

Curiously, no. The money doesn't seem real to me. It might seem a lot more real when the Woolwich come knocking on my door, asking for their money back, admittedly, but at the moment it's just like one big game of Monopoly.

Mayfair, here I come!

PS: Recommended Autonomy to Richard but he wasn't impressed. The current price is roughly £60 per share. 'I think it's peaked,' he said.

Thursday, 3 February

22.00: Just got back from a party at the Harbour Club in Chelsea. Sally invited me. She's a member there. We played tennis first and she wore a very tight white Lycra outfit which showed off everything to very good effect. She is one of those people to whom looking good is every bit as important as playing good.

The party was not my scene: if the Harbour Club was a magazine it would be *Hello!* (and most definitely not the *Big Issue*).

Sally went off to flirt with the tennis coaches so I sat in the corner counting toupees and face-lifts and the odd B- and C-grade celeb.

The Harbour Club is a bit of a magnet for celebs, actually: Princess Diana used to be a member. (It was where she picked up Will Carling with the line 'What does a girl have to do to get a coffee round here?')

Tonight Ainsley Harriott was wandering around. A friend of Sally's introduced us but I could tell he wasn't remotely interested in talking to me so I cut it short by going to the bog. Mid-slash I decided to leave. On the way out I saw Sally, beaming, surrounded by three good-looking blokes. I didn't want to disturb her so I didn't bother saying goodbye.

Friday, 4 February

One of the biggest problems I am coming across is information overload. I am drowning. We all need information to be able to invest wisely, but where do we start, with so many frigging outlets to choose from?

OK, the *FT* is recognised as one of the best sources, but easy to read it ain't. I have, however, managed to get the sense of some articles, by employing the same tactics that I used to use for those optical illusion pictures that were all the rage in the *Daily Mail* magazine a couple of years ago: they looked like shapeless messes of colour at first, but if you stared long enough, and concentrated, eventually images that made some kind of sense would emerge.

Apart from the *FT*, it seems there are millions of newspapers, radio programmes, newsletters, TV shows and websites out there, all offering you financial information. There are even entire TV channels dedicated to it, for Christ's sake! It's all very over-whelming. I've tried to make some sense of it all at the back of this book. Anyway, today I tried to make my Big Purchase of Autonomy shares over the Internet.

Ironically, given the title of this book, I couldn't: because share trading on-line is still a relatively new phenomenon here, there are still loads of companies whose shares aren't yet linked up to the system. Autonomy is one of them: it's quoted not on the London Stock Market but on a market called the EASDAQ, which has only come into existence recently.

The EASDAQ (It stands for 'European Association of Securities Dealers Automated Quotes') is for companies who are growing dead quickly, who want to raise money from investors all over Europe.

The story of EASDAQ is interesting. (God, I'd never have

found myself saying that two months ago.) It started because the traditional old buffers on the London Stock Market wouldn't let the likes of Autonomy in, because they couldn't come up with the necessary paperwork: anyone joining had to show the stock market prefects three years' worth of accounts. For Autonomy, who were just two years old when they wanted to join, that was a bit difficult.

So the bright sparks at EASDAQ (based in Brussels) nipped in to fill the void.

Mind you, as far as trading EASDAQ shares on the Net goes, things change very fast in cyberland: by the time this book is published, I'm sure it'll be much easier.

So I've had to send off for an order form, from a City stock-broking firm. This is how things used to get done, before the Net arrived: anyone who wanted to buy and sell stocks and shares themselves would have to sign up as a private client with some snotty stockbroking company. If the stockbroking company would deign to let them on board, that is.

In a way, I prefer buying shares like this: when you get them over the Net it somehow doesn't seem real, and you worry that the whole system might just crash one day, taking all your money, which you'll never see again, with it.

Anyway, I have decided on my strategy. Day trading – i.e. buying shares in the morning and selling them the same day – is for goons, I have decided. The figures prove it, too: 70% of all day traders end up losing money. Instead, I will back Autonomy big time – i.e. to the tune of 30k – through thick and thin, for the whole of this year. I have also bunged bundles of 2,500k on eight other shares I like the look of and I will stick with them too.

Here are the eight:

1) **Charlton Athletic.**

For the simple reason that I support them. 'A love bet', as

Sally calls it. If you fancy investing in a football club, though, beware: in general (with one obvious exception) they are not a good bet. Footie clubs, in the main, are not dynamic money-making propositions. This is because of their huge wage bills: the higher the salaries, the lower the profits. In hard business terms, footie clubs are often vanity objects – rich men's playthings.

Often, the rich men come to realise that what they have bought is nothing more than a very expensive 11-man money-shredder (albeit one that gives them a great deal of pleasure). Take Fulham, and Mohamed Al Fayed, for example: he paid £30 million for the club and currently it's losing him £8 million a year. Ditto Ken Bates, at Chelsea: the wages there are so high it's rumoured that even the hot-dog salesman is on ten grand a week.

With Charlton, I'm not being completely driven by my emotions, though. They look like a very good bet for promotion to the Premier League. If that happens they will be playing in front of far bigger crowds, and getting a good slice of the TV millions as well. At present they're worth around £25 million on the stock market, but if you tot up the value of all the players and the ground it would come to a lot more than that. As the season goes on, I reckon, more people will buy into them, so the more the price will go up.

One team that *is* a money-making machine, of course, is Manchester United. And they have the potential to make even more. They are so huge, worldwide, it's not true. The other day they advertised a competition on the Internet. In Thailand alone, one million people applied.

That last figure will make very depressing reading for a bloke called Michael Knighton. A few years ago he tried to buy United. To secure the deal, he needed to raise just

£5 million. But no one would lend it to him. Which, for him, was a pity: the club is now worth more than a billion.

2) **Monotub**.

A friend of mine, who works for an advertising agency, has told me that her colleagues are all getting a bit excited about a new account they're working on. It's for a 'revolutionary' washing machine, to be launched later this year, called 'The Titan'. Apparently it will do for washing machines what the Dyson did for vacuum cleaners. Monotub make it.

What's great about it, so I'm told, is that a) it's 'sexy', b) it takes a much bigger load than normal machines do, c) you can stop it in the middle of a wash and d) you don't have to touch your dirty laundry any more as the Titan comes complete with a laundry basket which you actually slot into the machine. Sounds worth a punt to me.

I did wonder if this came into the category of 'Insider Information', but having looked into it, it's nothing of the sort. Insider Information is, basically, when an officer of a company gives you secret information about that company, which could affect its share price.

My mate doesn't work for Monotub, for a kick-off, and the info about the Titan was hardly secret, as she showed me a newspaper article about it. But while we're on the subject, insider information is another area which is beginning to fascinate me. This is because – it seems to me – it's clearly an activity which completely disproves the saying 'Crime Doesn't Pay'. Everyone knows it happens (usually on the golf course. . . 'I shouldn't be telling you this, old boy, but . . .'), yet because it's so difficult to prove, there have been hardly any successful prosecutions.

A classic Insider Information scenario might be when, say, a politician gets told by his wife, in bed, that the company of which she is a director is about to be taken over. That is information which would have a huge upwards impact on the share price. If the politician then bought some shares in said company, that might be a Suitable Case For Investigation, but the chances of getting a conviction would be slight, given that it would depend on the wife testifying against her husband, in court.

Even accusing someone of insider trading (as opposed to bringing charges against them) is fraught with difficulty: a TV programme announced it was going to do just that, in November 1999. The show was going to be presented by a bloke who takes his shirt off a lot, and says unintentionally hilarious things like 'This is not about journalism. It is much bigger than that. Journalism is not a big enough word to describe what I do', but guess what: it didn't get transmitted.

3) **Airtel**.

They are developing a business which enables punters to use the Internet when they're on a plane. Sounds like a good idea to me, mate. I have this vision of a jumbo jet full of passengers logging on to a screen embedded in the back of the seat just in front of them.

4) **4Front Technologies.**

I am putting £2,500 into this on the basis that I like the company's name. Yes, I know this goes against every sensible rational investment rule there is, but as my mate Isaac said to me the other day: 'In the current climate, the less rational you are the more likely you are to make money.' This is an experiment, after all, so I want to try out irrational methods of investment as well as sane ones.

4Front, like Autonomy, is quoted on the EASDAQ: I've noticed their share price go up steadily in the last few days, and I want to join the party. It's as simple, and as stupid, as that.

I also like the fact that the company, owing to the fact

that its name starts with a 4, is the first to be quoted on the EASDAQ list, even before those companies that start with the letter 'A'. It reminds me of a tactic used by my mum. She used to run a bed-and-breakfast place in Sutton, in South London, in the 80s. (She was so keen to make money I would sometimes come home late at night and find she'd let my bedroom to a stranger.) She was determined that her place would always be the first entry in the local Yellow Pages, under the entries for guest houses. So she called it 'A and B Bed and Breakfast Guest House'.

In the next edition, though, someone called their gaff 'AA Guest House', thus relegating Mum to second place. She retaliated by inserting so many 'A's' into her next entry ('AAAAAAAAAA Guest House') that whoever was trying to compete with her suddenly realised what they were up against, and gave up.

I don't even know what 4Front do. I don't even want to know. I don't even know if the CEO has a beard. But I want to see whether it's possible to make money on the basis of sticking a pin in the paper, with your eyes shut.

5) **Transense.**

This lot make electronic chip type things for cars. When the tyres are about to burst they will make a sign on your dashboard go 'beep beep'. The plan, it seems, is to have them fitted as standard, to just about every car in the world. This makes them a good bet, in my book.

6) **Monticello**.

As recommended to me by Big Kev, a bloke with a very large belly, whom I met the other night at the Wimbledon dog track. He works in the City (not for Monticello, though) and says there's going to be an announcement very soon which will send the price over the crossbar and into the stands. His mate, he says, is so confident he's put £150,000 into it.

Is taking tips from fat blokes at the greyhounds the way to
Make A Million? I feel I should invest £2,500 to find out.

7) **MV Sports**.

This lot are run by David Lloyd, the ex-tennis player.
Apparently they have the rights to a lot of Buzz Lightyear
mechandise. Buzz is the animated star of *Toy Story 2*, which
everyone reckons is going to be the must-see kids' movie
of the year.

8) **Birchin International**.

They specialise in training Net dunces, i.e. Telling them how
to use the Internet. That's a big market.

Here we go!

Sunday, 6 February

Went to a party thrown by Richard (Normal) at his place in
Norbiton last night. Halfway through I realised I am still very
much turning into the kind of person I used to detest. All I talked
about was the stockmarket. I couldn't help it: it has begun to
fascinate me. I hope I don't end up like Gollum in Tolkein's *Lord
of the Rings*. He got more and more corrupted by the gold ring
he was wearing (the ring symbolised money) and in the end it
sent him potty and he fell down a big volcano. At one stage
Richard asked me, 'So what's your strategy, Jonny?'

He said it slightly sarcastically, and with a smile, so he might
have been taking the piss, but I answered him anyway. After a
few seconds, that is: I had to think about it.

'I'm bunging loads on one company and a fair bit on a few
others and I'm going to sit tight till the end of the year and clean
up.'

'Ah,' said Mark, my mate who works in the City but isn't a
wanker. 'Buy and hold.'

That made me feel quite good: I now have an officially
recognised investment strategy! Everyone needs a strategy – even

if it's based on buying into companies whose name starts with the letter 'B'. There are many different types of strategy, of course, and having spent all day reading about them I am now in a position to share them with you.

It's by no means a comprehensive list, but hopefully it'll get you thinking. I've also been thinking about Sally a fair bit.

Velda from two doors down is clearly dying for us to go out with each other and keeps tapping me for gossip. I've been round to Sally's to play Scrabble a lot recently, but Velda clearly thinks that's a cover story, and that we have in fact been having wild sex.

Well, we haven't. I can't say the thought of having wild sex with Sally appals me, mind you, but at my age (38 . . . I can't believe it) having wild sex with your neighbour, or attempting to, is not a sensible long-term strategy. So what is my (emotional, not financial) long-term strategy? Well, I'm not really in the right frame of mind to go out with anyone at the moment. I spent last year licking my wounds (and behaving irresponsibly) following the end of (yet another) failed relationship. However, I am beginning to see that there is something fundamentally attractive about Sally: she is a good person. A very good person. Anyone who can bring up two kids on their own, like she has, automatically becomes more attractive. It's about having a backbone, and being a survivor. Being tasty helps too, of course: and she is. Very.

But I just couldn't contemplate going out with her.

Anyway: here are ten investment theories (with an extra one for good measure).

1) Invest on the dips.

This is a system very much favoured by The Man In The Pub. And indeed The Man In The Bar, i.e. the average American investor. It involves tracking the price of a chosen share and lying in wait until the price dips. Then you pile in.

It has been working well for a lot of people, apparently: but the problem is that sometimes – particularly with Internet shares – it's not based on any sensible factors (the prospect of real long-term growth, for instance) but superficial ones.

It's a bit like backing West Ham to win the league just because they've won their last game. The reason it's been working for some is that if enough people do it, it becomes a self-fulfilling prophecy: when lots of people buy on a dip, the price will go up. Everyone will then go around with a smile on their face thinking they're brilliant investors, when, in reality, nothing has changed.

This system worries me. It might work occasionally, on a company whose share price you know intimately, but as a general rule of investment it seems less than sensible. (Yes, I know I've just invested £2,500 in a company solely on the basis that I like the sound of its name: do as I say, not as I do.) The big worry with this method is that you might end up investing in a company whose share price is plummeting for a very good reason: i.e. the chief executive has just been put away for fraud. In which case you would simply be throwing good money after bad, or 'catching a falling knife' as they say in the City. Backing a share in these circumstances is the equivalent of putting your money on a one-legged man to win an arse-kicking contest.

2) **Invest when it climbs**.

Again, quite popular with The Man In The Pub. Or, to be exact, The Man In The Pub Who Isn't Following Theory Number One.

This is also called 'momentum trading,' and the drawbacks are the same as those described above: i.e. often it works on the basis that it's a self-fulfilling prophecy.

A cricketing friend of mine, Thommo, a very big cheese in a very big IT company, and a former 'West Croydon

Young Businessman Of The Year', told me an interesting story the other day.

Sometimes, when a share, after much toing and froing, reaches a statistically significant point – 500p, let's say – it will then shoot up almost instantly, to, say, 675p.

This is because a lot of mega-billion-pound pension funds are partly controlled by computers. These computers are programmed to stock up on certain shares in certain sectors, but only at certain points. Now if that point is 500p: bingo.

At 499p that share might be classified by the computer as low priority; at 1p more, it could be medium priority, and as such an automatic buy. End result: lots of mega-billion-pound pension fund computers buy it, and the price shoots up.

There has been a lot of this 'momentum trading' recently, so I'm told: much to the exasperation of the City's Old Hands, who have made careers out of following my next theory, which is . . .

3) **Sensible Fundamental Analysis**.

This is a bit boring but it's by far and away the most low-risk approach: trouble is, in the current climate, as my mate Thommo says, being rational gets you nowhere. SFA involves looking at things like a company's balance sheets. Is the company making a profit? What products is it going to launch next year? Are they any good? Is the sector the company operates in likely to do well next year? The key statistic to look at here is something called the 'Price to Earnings Ratio'. This is very important, so pay attention. If you go round quoting what the City Boys call 'P/E ratios' all the time you may not know what you're talking about but you will certainly sound impressive. Which counts for a lot in the City.

P/E ratios can often be found in the *FT*, listed next to a company's share price. A small one – of, say, 7 – is low risk. A big one – 300 – is, SFA devotees will tell you, A Bloody Great Risk.

It works like this. Let's say a company's share price is £10. Let's say its earnings, proportionately, per share, are £1. That means its P/E ratio is 10 divided by 1: 10.

Worryingly, some Internet companies have no P/E ratios at all. This is because their earnings are so tiny – or, in some cases, non-existent. For many old buffer types in the City, investing in companies with no P/E ratios is madness. They keep quoting 'stock market legend' Daniel Drew's phrase: 'It's like buying cows by candlelight'.

They have a point, of course, especially when you realise that some of these new companies' 'earnings' are nothing of the sort: sometimes they will be a mirage. That's because some firms count as 'earnings' somebody else's advert on their website: even though that advert hasn't actually been paid for, in cash, at all. Often it will be there as part of a barter-type agreement with another website: 'You take a free advert on my site and I'll take one on yours'.

The more creative dotcom, however, will count that free advert as 'income' on the basis that it's worth – notionally – five grand, let's say. A bit naughty. The bad news for companies who do this is that the authorities are getting wise to it. At least they are in America, where there are now tough new guidelines about what firms can and can't count as 'earnings'.

Thommo, however (West Croydon Young Businessman Of The Year), maintains than the absence of P/E data is often nothing to worry about. He argues that when they found there was oil in the North Sea it took years for the real earnings to come through: but when they did . . . bingo. The longer the wait for real profits, he argues, the bigger those profits might be in the end.

The Thommos of this world seem to be having their day at the moment: which is why people who still preach the old SFA values of P/E ratios are being openly mocked in the street and, in some cases, sacked. (In fact, at least a couple of City fund managers have recently been told to get on their bikes for being seen as too old school.) I suspect their day will return.

4) Complicated mathematical formulae.

Apparently these can work for a short time but they're far too complex for the likes of you and me, and anyway, I was shit at maths at school so I wouldn't want to be entrusted with the task of explaining any of them to you.

The problem here is that once a formula becomes popular it stops working quite as well: mainly because if The Many are now following it, as opposed to The Few, it automatically becomes less effective.

Once, I'm told, there was a formula – code-name GARP – which had quite a few devotees: but I can't find anyone who knows exactly how it worked . . .

5) Use a dartboard.

There is a (possibly apocryphal) tale about a unit trust manager who used to select companies to invest in by throwing darts at a dartboard. In 1995, apparently, his portfolio won the award for 'Best Performance By A Unit Trust' at the City's Oscars.

Again, not the most sensible option, but right now . . . why not? My choice of 4Front Technologies as an investment vehicle could, I think, be classified as Dartboard Theory in action.

6) Chaos theory.

I'm told there are some analysts who liken predicting the stock market to forecasting the weather: there is no logic to what happens, just a series of apparently random events. If you approach things in the right way, it's argued, you can

make certain reasonably reliable forecasts. Not one for me,
I'm afraid.

7) Choose your sector and go for it.

This is finding a lot of favour at the moment. The TMT
(Technology, Media and Telecom) sector in particular. But
it's a dangerously general system to follow. You need to
distinguish between individual TMT companies. To invest
blindly in the TMT sector is a bit like assuming someone's
bound to be good at cricket just because they're Australian.

8) Sector rotation.

Not unlike 7), but different in that it involves predicting what
sector is going to be hot *before* it even starts simmering: and
then, when it's just about to boil over, transferring all your
dosh into what you think is going to be the Next Big Thing.

9) Chartism.

No, not the 18th (or was it 17th?) century political movement
but the art of predicting share prices by looking at graphs, or
charts. At its crudest, it can be explained thus: If a share graph
goes up and down a lot but its general trend is upward, as
below, then the company might well be a good bet:

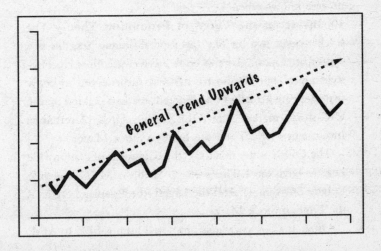

But if the reverse is true:

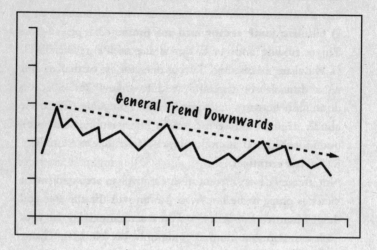

then steer clear. The trouble is, past performance is no guarantee of future performance: and anyway, at the moment, all the old tried and trusted tactics are being discarded as market conditions are unique.

Normal service may be resumed at some stage . . . but no one knows when.

10) **Invest on the Verge of Promotion Theory**. The stock market is a bit like the football league. Yes, this is a cynical attempt to give this book a *Fever Pitch* Nick Hornby-style appeal, but it's also true. It may surprise you to know that there are actually three different markets making up the UK stock market: the OFEX, the AIM, (Alternative Investment Market) and the London Stock Market.

The OFEX is the smallest – the equivalent of Nationwide League Division 2. The next up is the AIM (Nationwide League Division 1). And the largest, the Premier League, is the London Stock Market.

Often, if a company gets promoted from OFEX to AIM,

its share price rockets. This is because the next market up has a lot more (very rich) investors who do business in it. A bit like a footie team which gets promoted: it plays before bigger crowds (and gets a bigger slice of TV revenues).

If a share makes it to the big one, the list of the top 100 most valuable companies in the UK – the FOOTSIE 100, as it's known – there's an even better reason for its price to go up. This is because lots of big pension funds and institutions which do nothing but keep track of the FOOTSIE 100 ('Tracker Funds') have a policy of buying shares in every single company in that list, regardless. It's an accepted policy. So if a company looks like it's heading for the top 100, you might want to buy it. This is, to a certain extent, the same phenomenon that my mate Thommo was telling me about. Likewise, when a company drops out of the top 100, its price inevitably falls.

This is another good buying opportunity, as the share, at this lower price, may well then be a good-value bargain.

To make this system work for you, you should put money into a company just before it's going to be promoted, and then sell shortly after it's happened.

How do you know it's going to be promoted? Log on to any of the many financial websites listed at the end of this book, click on a company's name and read its literature. Often there will be a line in a news release somewhere, saying something like 'We are looking to go for an AIM listing in July'. Don't take their word for it, though: sometimes the listing never happens, or gets postponed, because of admin. problems, or a change in market conditions.

Alternatively, look in the *Investors Chronicle*. (Not the most exciting read in the world, it has to be said, but useful.)

This system seems to be working well for some people: at the moment anyway. A recent study showed that out of 32 companies promoted at the beginning of this year, 30 saw their share prices increase (sometimes dramatically) on the day of promotion.

A word of warning about OFEX, though: it's *very* volatile and there is an element of goalpost changing, when it comes to the rules of buying and selling. This is because the blokes who control OFEX market prices are at liberty to decide, quite arbitrarily, that they won't let you sell your shares at the price you *think* you're going to get: i.e. the publicly quoted one.

Let's say you've bought 10,000 shares in an OFEX company, at 100p each. Then the price falls to 80p and you want to get rid of them, quick. But the trader in charge of those shares might say to you: 'Blimey, because this is a small company, there are only 20,000 shares in it: if I sell 10,000 at 80p it may be that no one will want to buy them back at that price: Sorry, mate, if you want to sell 10,000, I'll give you 80p for half of them, but only 60p for the other half.' Quite legitimate and a bit of a sickener.

10a) **Follow a tip from a bloke in the pub or a taxi driver**. Or indeed a bloke called Big Kev at the Wimbledon dog track. Just to see what happens.

Tuesday, 8 February

Some people are really lucky: their hobby is their work. I mean, look at Keith Richards, for example. All he's ever wanted to do is take industrial quantities of drugs, play the guitar, and have a Very Good Time Indeed. And that's what he's done, for the last 40 odd years: it's his job. Ditto Ian Botham. Except for drugs and music, read cricket, and going off on ludicrously long charity walks piss-ups. Lucky git. I would have loved to have followed in either of their footsteps but never had a chance, owing to a phenomenal lack of sporting and musical talent.

Today, however, I came as close to that as I'm ever likely to, because Jeff, my boss at *Tonight with Trevor McDonald*, has asked me to do a TV report on . . . people who buy and sell stocks and shares over the Internet. For once, this is a subject I know more about than the researcher.

Most people don't realise, but so-called 'investigative' TV reporters actually do very little investigation at all: they have teams of researchers and producers to do it for them. That's not to say they are useless, disposable bolt-ons: a good TV reporter will stamp his or her identity on the piece, and make it theirs. Their job is to write or rewrite the script, and try and bring the piece to life. (And, if they're lucky, as a bonus, they'll get lumped by an irate interviewee: it makes great TV.) The most difficult bit, though, is to try and communicate, simply, directly and (if appropriate) entertainingly, what the thing is all about, to the most important person of all: the viewer. Some people are great at this: John Simpson, for example. Others aren't. Witness the legion of robotic staccato-toned stiffs who clog up the BBC News every day.

The report I've started today will take three or four days to film, and will consist mainly of interviews with people who have given up their jobs to trade on-line. There will also be tips, from experts, the first of whom, Adam Faith, I interviewed today. I met him at the headquarters of his new project: Moneyworld, a new satellite TV channel, which is based on an industrial estate in London's Canary Wharf. Adam claims it's the first TV channel entirely dedicated to money matters, aimed squarely at the average punter. Other financial TV stations, like Bloomberg, he says, are niche products aimed at the more sophisticated (and richer) investor. I watched a bit of Moneyworld's output while I was waiting to meet Adam. A bloke called Gavin Campbell, formerly

of Esther Rantzen's *That's Life*, and several seaside Xmas panto-
mimes, was presenting. Clearly, it's not going to be the kind of
station that people watch all day: it's a dip-in-and-out job. In the
bit I saw, six barrow-boy-type blokes discussed the price of a
share, somewhere in the City, for three minutes. Then there was
an interview with a bloke wearing glasses. He seemed to know
what he was talking about. Every so often a share price graph
would flash up on the screen. Two months ago I wouldn't have
given this kind of thing one millisecond: yet here I was, strangely
compelled, actually watching, and understanding. Truly, Lord, I
am learning a new language.

I was taken into a small glass-fronted lounge-type area to meet
Adam. He was small, casually dressed and with thick, silvery hair.

He smiled a lot and kept calling me 'kid' (a good tactic: Anne
Robinson, whom I used to work with on *Watchdog*, and still have
nightmares about, used to call people 'kiddo' rather than run the
risk of getting someone's name wrong).

Adam was poor when he was a kid but he's not now. Through
his shares in Moneyworld alone (the concept was mainly his idea)
he's worth £15 million. On paper, that is: as a director of the
company, he can't cash his shares in till this time next year. He
won't be able to cash them in all at once either. As he explained,
if an important officer of a company sells too many of their shares
at once, questions get asked by other shareholders. Like: 'How
can we have confidence in this company if one of the big cheeses
is trying to lessen his stake in it? Why should we stay in if he's
getting out?' Likewise, he said, if directors suddenly start buying
shares in their own companies, that's often a sign that Very Good
Things are just around the corner.

Adam first got hooked on the stock market when he was 19
(more than 40 years ago). He bought some shares in the Rank
Organisation ('they cost twelve shillings and sixpence each').
Previously, he'd been into gambling, but once he started punting

on the stock market he realised this was a far more sensible way
to indulge his risk-taking habit.

Adam (real name Terence Nelhams, from Acton) has had quite
a life. He was a pop star in the 60s. His first hit was called 'What
Do You Want If You Don't Want Money?' In the 70s he turned
to acting. He played the title role in the TV series *Budgie* (in the
title sequence he ran, in slow motion, through hundreds of
banknotes swirling around in the breeze) and also starred opposite David Essex in one of the great rock films of all time, *Stardust*
(in which, in a quite uncalled-for act of wanton savagery, he killed
David's pet dog).

But things really took off for him (financially, that is) when
he started a column on personal finance for the *Mail on Sunday*:
someone had seen him on TV, reviewing a programme about
money, and reckoned his plain-speaking style would translate
well on to the page. And it did. Offers started coming in: soon
he found himself a partner in an investment company. It hasn't
all been plain sailing, though: at one stage, owing to some unfortunate investment decisions, the fortune that Adam had been
steadily accruing all but disappeared. He argues that's made him
an even better investor: 'If you can keep your head while all
around you are losing theirs, etc.' We ended up filming the interview slap bang in front of a massive Moneyworld logo: he refused
to do it anywhere else. He is nothing if not canny: he knew that
if we'd done it where we wanted to (i.e. on the studio floor,
which would have looked a lot better on TV) he wouldn't have
got a massive subliminal plug in for the station. And it didn't
end there: during the interview he must have mentioned
Moneyworld about 40 times. The bit we are going to use,
however, doesn't feature the 'M' word. It's the bit where he gives
us his basic investment philosophy.

Which, put simply, is this: go down the pub. Adam favours the
commonsense approach: the pub, he says, is often a highly fertile

source of valuable investment information. If you're having a drink with your mate, and he's, say, an engineer, and he's saying, 'Bloody hell, I'm out on my feet, we've been working so hard,' then a little light bulb should flick on in your head. If he's that knackered, his company must have a lot of work on. Which means they might be a good investment bet. Likewise, if you see a café that's always full, and it's part of a chain, why not investigate further? It all sounded pretty sensible to me: especially when he banged on about doing your homework. And most importantly of all, he said it in a simple chatty way that will make good TV. I couldn't resist it: before leaving, I asked if he fancied resurrecting his singing career with my band, Surf 'n' Turf. 'Nah, kid. Sorry. Don't like pop music. Never have done.'

Wednesday, 9 February

19.00: I am in a hotel in Leeds suffering from SPWS (Share Price Withdrawal Syndrome). I'm nowhere near my computer so the only thing I can do is check CEEFAX, which isn't ideal, as it has only a limited number of shares quoted on it. Which is why, earlier on today, I rang my mate Mark who works in the City (but isn't a wanker) four times for price quotes.

I needn't have bothered: nothing much has been happening. It's a good job we've known each other 27 years (we were at school together) as anyone else would have got well pissed off with that level of financial stalking. Mark is an interesting barometer of what's happened to me: he is a very gentle, kind, placid bloke – completely unlike the stereotypical, arrogant City types – whose generous proportions call to mind a thirtysomething Billy Bunter.

We've always been close, but for the last 15 years we've hardly ever talked about each other's jobs: I thought his was boring and impenetrable and morally vacuous, he felt much the same about mine. Now, rather wonderfully, we have added another layer to our friendship: I can't stop talking to him about the City.

He thinks my about-turn is hilarious. What I've found out over the past few weeks is that I've been wrong to dismiss people in the City as wankers, who are in it just to make money. OK a lot of them are, but for many it's as much about ideas as it is dosh. There is nothing more exciting than seeing an idea for a business take wing, or seeing your judgment on a particular share vindicated. (Not that it's happened to me yet.)

Today I met two of those people who've given up their jobs to trade full time. The first was Martin Cockerill. He is an ex-gravy mix salesman from Leeds. If I thought I had it bad, Martin's got it worse. I, at least, have another job to keep me occupied: Martin doesn't. His only social outlet, apart from trading, is helping to run the local girls' under-12 football team. And guess what. The coach, the trainer and most of the parents trade as well, so all they ever end up talking about is . . . shares. They've formed an investment club together: they all put in £500 and meet every week to discuss what to do with it. These clubs are becoming increasingly popular and are a very good way to learn about the stock market gradually, without getting your fingers burned. But Martin isn't content with just being in an investment club. I met him at his house on the outskirts of the city. It was one of those rather soulless 80s jobs that, curiously, now seem far more dated than ones built several decades earlier.

After selling the real thing for a few years he tried to get on a different kind of gravy train: the property market. He did well in the 80s, but in the 90s, when the property and rental market collapsed, he decided to play the stock market. Like a lot of traders, he got hooked after experiencing an early windfall. A toy company whose shares he'd invested in heavily went up 500% in ten days. He made £30,000. That was it. Previously he'd done his research by Teletext but now he switched to the Internet. It doesn't seem to have done him much good, though: in the weeks following that big payday, he lost that entire £30,000. Since then, he has painstakingly earned it back. He argues that he's on course for a yearly income of well over forty grand, so he's still feeling pretty pleased with himself.

I don't think he was taking into account the costs of trading, though. Rather like me, last month, he was getting so caught up in the excitement of it all that he was forgetting to account for the fact that a single trade can cost up to £15 a time: and he's been doing up to 12 trades a day.

His life now totally revolves around trading. He gets up at 7.30, heads straight for his computer, and reads as much as he can, from various financial websites. He's developed his own little book of rules: he doesn't buy before 8.15 but he might sell. He tends to cash in his chips sooner rather than later if he's sitting on a profit. He reckons he's only in it for a year: then he's going to get out.

Martin's wife, Helen, a former nurse, is also hooked. She does a lot of his research for him, and is always making recommend-ations. Unfortunately, he doesn't take much notice of her. She strongly backed an Internet company called Affinity a few months back, when they were about a quid a share: he didn't bite. Right now, they're £70 a go. If he'd put in £10,000 – not an unusual sum for him to invest – he'd be pushing millionaire status.

After the interview we went to film him coaching the girls' football team, the Leeds Vixens Under-12s. Once the cameras stopped rolling we challenged the girls to a game: me, Jim the director, Gurbir the researcher and Mike the cameraman (and his son, who was doing the sound).

They beat us 4–3. (Their tactics reminded me of the Leeds team from the early 70s . . . lots of shirt-tugging, and some brutal tackles from behind. Vixens indeed.)

Also, met Sally Mitchell. She's in her fifties, and owns a company specialising in fine art prints of animals. Her dog prints, apparently, are world famous. She doesn't actually run the firm any more, though: trading has taken her life over so much she's handed over day-to-day control of the business to her son.

Her life has taken one almighty – and quite unexpected – twist. She now spends up to twelve hours a day in front of her computer, researching shares, and poring over her portfolio.

What struck me about Sally was that she was such an eminently sensible person. I had expected on-line traders to be greedy loadsamoney types with pound signs in their bulging eyes. But Sally was level-headed, and honest. Yes, she'd had bad days: once she'd fallen for the charms of the wrong company, and lost £12,000 overnight. What happened to her should be a lesson for everyone: she had fallen for what is known as a 'pump-and-dump', or 'ramping'. This is when someone starts singing the praises of a particular company, usually on an Internet bulletin board, with the aim of making a quick profit. Often the pump-and-dumper will use less than subtle language with lots of exclamation marks (e.g. 'THIS ONE IS GOING ALL THE WAY!!!! FILL YOUR BOOTS NOW!!!'). Sometimes they will be a little more sophisticated, but the modus operandi is the same: the pump-and-dumper will have bought lots of the shares (usually cheap ones, costing 10p or less) before they post up their messages. Then, once unsuspecting members of the public like Sally pile in, the pumper sells – i.e. dumps – and makes a huge profit.

Pump-and-dumpers are the scourge of Internet trading . . . they are cyberhighwaymen. It was bound to happen: they are preying on our greed and ignorance. The trouble is, it's incredibly hard to catch them: if someone mugs you, at least the police have clues to go on. This lot, literally, operate in space. The Financial Services Authority, whose job it is to protect investors' interests, are supposed to bring pump-and-dumpers to book: but the time/money/logistical constraints are huge.

So, in the end, it's up to us. The best way to avoid being a victim of this kind of thing is, I think, never to believe anything you read, without checking it first. If someone says The Great Shoe Company Ltd from Braintree in Essex is in merger talks, try ringing them up yourself: if you ask nicely they might well tell you. Or, in extreme circumstances, if the information written is libellous and potentially detrimental to the share price (i.e. a reverse pump-and-dump), they could take action to have it expunged from the Net.

Despite her unfortunate experience, Sally says that overall she's doing well: she's made a 70% profit in the last six months. She is now making more from shares than she was from her business.

'I get a fantastic buzz from it,' she said. 'I can't stop.'

I wonder if she'll be singing the same tune in ten months. I must remember to call her.

Thursday, 10 February

Here's a question for you: what have Katrina and the Waves and the Brotherhood Of Man got in common? You've got ten seconds.

If you answered 'They both won the Eurovision Song Contest, the former with "Love Shine A Light", the latter with "Save All Your Kisses For Me",' you would only have been half right. Because fascinatingly (well, for me anyway) the full answer is that both groups contain members who are avid on-line traders.

I know this because I interviewed them both today for my report. I met Vince and Alex, from the Waves, at a rehearsal studio on a farm near Cambridge. Vince was a spiky American, Alex was tall, well preserved, stringy and posh. The best bit was when they let me play along with them to their biggest hit, 'Walking On Sunshine'. We needed some general shots to glue the different bits of interview together – visual cement if you like.

For two weeks in the early 80s I did nothing but listen to 'Walking On Sunshine': it felt like they had captured joy, in a bottle, and then recorded it. And here I was, playing it (badly) with them! God, it was good.

Anyway, as for their trading, they've both been doing well, they claim. Alex scared me a bit, though. He has been dealing in sums of over £100,000. He knows you shouldn't invest what you can't afford to lose, he says, but he really doesn't think it's possible to lose a sum as large as that. I'm not so sure.

But there really is something happening out there: when complete novices are investing such almighty sums on the basis of a perceived gold rush, the chances of it ending in tears (or a few, at least) must be high. I hope he's going to be OK. Then again maybe they really do know want they're doing: another call in ten months' time, methinks.

The other bloke we interviewed, Roger Pritchard from the Brotherhood of Man (their heavy-metal death anthem 'Save Your Kisses For Me' won Eurovision in the early 70s), claims he'd made close to a million pounds last year. We couldn't trawl his accounts to see if he really had, but the beatific smile permanently on his face suggested that he had indeed been enjoying himself recently. And there really is no doubt that an awful lot of people out there have been making an awful lot of money recently. I wonder if I can be one of them.

The trouble is, what goes up must come down: will an awful lot of people out there soon start to lose an awful lot of money? And will I be one of them?

Friday, 11 February

Went round to Sally's for dinner. There should be a sign on her door saying 'Steaks R Us'. She grilled four T-bones, which I thought was a bit excessive given that it was just me, her, Luke (11) and Sophie (8). I needn't have worried: Sophie methodically worked her way through the entire slab of beef, and a jacket potato, before moving serenely on to profiteroles and cream. It was a remarkable sight. I don't know where she puts it: there isn't an ounce of fat on her. It's great to see a little girl with such a stupendous appetite. She really is a sweetie.

At one stage I found myself looking – staring, really – at Sally while she gazed at Sophie in that loving, proud way mothers do. Quite attractive, really.

Anyway, it's now a week since I invested my 50k. And I'm feeling pretty pleased with myself. This is how things look, after Week One of the Experiment Proper:

NAME OF CO.	INITIAL STAKE	SHARE PRICE THEN	SHARE PRICE NOW	WHAT'S MY STAKE WORTH NOW, THEN?
Autonomy	£30,000	£58.55	£64.60	£32,300
Charlton	£2,500	54p	56p	£2,550
MV Sports	£2,500	4p	4p	£2,500
Birchin	£2,500	12p	12p	£2,500
Transense	£2,500	£7.95	£7.95	£2,500
4Front	£2,500	£14.90	£15.10	£2,540
Airtel	£2,500	38p	36p	£2,460
Monotub	£2,500	£2.70	£2.94	£2,620
Monticello	£2,500	£1.10	£1.10	£2,500
TOTAL	£50,000			£52,470

(I've rounded off all the totals to the nearest £10.)

And this is how the house looks:

Local estate agent (with briefcase) who is carrying out a valuation, as I am seriously considering moving to £1,000,000 house (which I will buy with my impending fortune) complete with gym and 'Surf 'n' Turf' rehearsal studio

And the publishers have insisted I do a share graph too, so here goes:

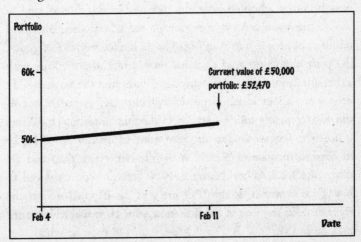

Portfolio

60k

Current value of £50,000
portfolio: £52,470

50k

Feb 4   Feb 11

Date

Meanwhile I have hit on a new wheeze – magnificent and totally legitimate – which, I reckon, is going to make me so much money that all my other share dealing antics will become quite redundant. It is a wonderful feeling and so easy I can't believe other people aren't doing it as well.

It's all about three simple letters: I, P and O. If you can get in big time on an IPO, that's it: at the moment, apparently, people are making zillions out of them. It stands for Initial Public Offering: this is when a company goes to the public, to try to raise stacks of money.

First off, the company will offer to sell a limited number of shares to a limited number of people in the know, i.e. big financial institutions. They might offer, say, a million shares, at one quid each: if they're all snapped up, the company will have successfully raised a million quid.

The fun starts when those shares are then made available to everyone: i.e. when they're floated on the stock market. On day one of a flotation, any old Tom, Dick and Harry can then get their hands on them. What was previously a limited, precious commodity, available only to a limited, precious number of people, now becomes a limited, precious commodity available to (and, at the moment, wanted by) everyone. As we know, when unlimited numbers of people start wanting to buy a limited number of goods, the price shoots up. And so it has proved recently: anything with a dotcom in its name, in fact anything with even the faintest whiff of dotcom about it, has gone through the roof. A classic case of this is a company called Oxygen (a dotcom outfit, natch). When it floated a few weeks ago its price went up on day one from 2p to 65p: an increase of 3000%. A slightly better rate than you get down the local Abbey National. Now, let's say you managed to buy £1,000 worth, at the IPO price of 2p: if you'd sold at the right time on day one of the floatation, your 1k would have turned into more than 30k. Brilliant! Money for old rope or what!

Unfortunately, I missed out on the Oxygen party: but I am going to get in on the next one, with a vengeance. A company called Interactive Investor International (iii) are floating very soon, and I've applied for £5,000 worth of shares. The application process is simple. All you do is:

1) Find out which companies are IPO-ing. A lot of IPOs are advertised in the press. Alternatively, buy the *Mail on Sunday*: their finance section lists forthcoming IPOs. When you apply, you will be sent . . .

2) A prospectus. Company prospectuses are the most boring pieces of literature on earth. Very few normal people bother to read them and the few that do haven't a clue what they're on about anyway. The prospectus contains page upon page of legal and financial small print and, crucially, a description of what the company does. Then:

3) Fill in the application form attached to the prospectus, send off your cheque, sit back and wait, and a couple of weeks later . . . bingo! Free money. Thank you very much.

I'm assuming that my iii shares will go up only a modest amount on day one. Let's say there will be a twenty-fold increase, compared to Oxygen's thirty-fold one. I won't be complaining: my five grand will have turned into a hundred grand, in a day. Easy or what!

Saturday, 12 February
I've been smiling all day: as you'd expect when you know anything up to a hundred grand is coming your way.

To celebrate I went for a curry with Mark (non-wanker City mate) at the Akash. I go there one to three times a week and am on first-name terms with all the waiters. They call me 'Mr Jonny' and always give me the table next to the fish tank (The Much Prized Seat Next To The Aquarium). The sign in the window says 'Akash Tandoori: one of the best Indian restaurants in Clapham Junction' (not hard – there are only three).

On the way back we had a rather symbolic moment; Mark stood under the streetlamp at the end of my road, and talked.

He had been in the City for nearly 20 years, he said, and he didn't understand what was going on. The sector he had been in for most of that time – banking – was getting hammered: some banks' share prices had halved in the last six months. And yet these were solid, reliable, well-known companies, with huge profits. Meanwhile, he said, all these new Internet companies, which had no track record and no profits, were booming. He was 'old economy', he said, and quite frankly he couldn't quite come to grips with the 'new economy', i.e. the Internet and all that hi-tech stuff. It was all rather poignant: he looked a little lost.

Sunday, 13 February

More evidence of my increasingly unhealthy obsessional (nay, antisocial) behaviour: tonight, Surf 'n' Turf played 'A Pre-Valentine's Night Special' at Numero Uno, the Italian bistro down the road. Just as Jackie our singer was coming to the most emotional bit of 'Walk On By', I asked Richard (Normal), loudly, over her shoulder, whether he'd applied for shares in iii.

Our guitarist Matt (who is also the co-presenter of BBC1's *Weekend Watchdog* and therefore, like me, a grade-D celeb – i.e. people vaguely recognise you but they don't know what you do) was not amused and bollocked me, for behaviour unbecoming to a 'professional' musician. Given that we have the 'Proper music played by professionals' tag to live up to, I think he had a point.

Sally came along too: she is dead sociable. Whenever I looked up from my bass (not often: I'm so shit I spend most of time with my eyes glued to the fretboard) I saw her laughing/drinking/chatting.

She is definitely quite tasty but I'm definitely not interested.

Monday, 14 February

I read a story today which, for a few seconds, made me want to give up this whole project for good. It was about an American bloke called Mark Barton, a day trader from Atlanta. He wasn't very good. He was hooked on volatile hi-tech shares, and like the rest of us amateurs had absolutely no experience of the world he was entering. His problem, apparently, was that he confused a share's past performance with what it was likely to do in the future. It got him into big trouble. Early in 1999 his on-line brokers closed his account, as he'd lost $400,000. But that didn't stop him: he opened another one just across the road. Then things got worse: in just two weeks he lost another $100,000. One night he went home and beat his wife's head in with a hammer, stuck her head under water, and threw her in the closet. The following night he killed his three children. The next day he walked into two 'trading shops' and shot nine day traders dead before turning the gun on himself.

It would be too simplistic to say that day trading made Mark Barton commit murder: clearly, he was a 24-carat nutter before he went anywhere near the stock market. But day trading was the spark that made his deranged mind blow: volatile markets and even more volatile minds make a dangerous combination.

Tuesday, 15 February

Now about that free money. You know, the IPO thing. It hasn't quite worked out the way I expected. I should have known, of course – no such thing as a free lunch, etc., etc. What's happened is that so many people have applied for shares in iii, everyone's getting far less than they asked for. I wanted £5,000 worth: I'm getting less than a tenth of that. That got me thinking: how much money are iii making out of the likes of me?

I've done the sums, and the results are revealing: this whole IPO exercise has been quite a nice little earner for iii.

The offer was *thirteen* times oversubscribed by ordinary private investors like you and me: 82,000 of us applied for shares. Unfortunately iii won't tell me how much money those 82,000 sent in between them, but let's assume the average cheque was for £1,000 (not unreasonable: the minimum you could apply for was £500 worth). That means iii are now sitting on 82,000 × £1,000: £82,000,000. That's now in a bank account, earning iii interest of up to £150,000 a week. Mind you, that figure could be higher. When I asked the company to confirm it, they wouldn't: they said the relevant information wasn't in the public domain.

Hmmmm. iii have done absolutely nothing wrong: they are only doing exactly what the big utility companies did in the 80s, when gas, water and electricity privatisations were all the rage. They've been completely open about it too: they told everyone what they were doing in their prospectus.

Even so, it makes you think: iii's big slogan, their selling point, is the rather enticing 'FINANCIAL POWER IS CHANGING HANDS'. The inference is that now at last, thanks to the Internet, we, the Great Unwashed, can share in the spoils of capitalism.

I'm not so sure. At the moment, real financial power is still very much in the hands of the likes of iii, methinks.

Wednesday, 16 February

I know I said I'd chosen my strategy and I was sticking to it but today, on the train up to Manchester, I read an article in the *FT* that made me do a small U-turn. Sorry. The gist of the piece was that 'Business To Consumer' (B2C) Internet outfits were no longer attracting the smart money. Oh no. Business To Business (B2B) is where it's at.

What the hell am I talking about? Well, here goes:

Up until now, B2C Internet companies have been getting a very good press. And very high share ratings. They specialise in selling goods or services directly to the consumer, e.g. Last-minute.com (holidays, hotel bookings, meals, etc.) and Amazon (books, CDs). But now, 'experts' are starting to cotton on to the fact that the pavements in B2C land aren't made of solid gold. Running a Business to Consumer outfit is fraught with logistical difficulties. Like getting the right goods to the right people at the right time. Once you've taken those costs into account, the profit margins on things like books and CDs aren't great.

B2B is different, apparently. Here, there's no mucking about delivering a piddly pair of trainers to someone in Norwich – it's just big savings and big profits all the way. The B2B thing is all about business using the Internet to deal with other businesses. Let's say you're a steel company and you want to buy £10 million worth of the stuff. Being sensible, you'd want to check steel prices all round the world. *Before* the Internet, you'd have had to wait weeks/months to get all the quotes in.

Now, the theory goes, you can get virtually instant quotes (and instant virtual ones) from all over the world, at the push of a button.

You just log on to steelquotes.com, or whatever, put up a sign saying 'I want a million tons of steel, anyone who's interested e-mail me now', and then sit back and wait for the best bid.

It's easy, it's quick, and it could save you millions and millions. So. B2B is in! B2C is out! And guess what: a UK B2B business floated on the stock exchange this very day: it's called just2clicks.com and it's been getting very good reviews. One of the blokes behind it, Karl Watkin, has apparently seen his initial investment of £2,500 turn into a million, on paper, overnight.

I wanted to invest £2,500 too, but I had no money left: my £50,000 was all tied up. The only option was to sell something, so, arbitrarily, I picked Transense, the lot that put warning chips in tyres. I phoned a stockbroker to ask him to do both trades for me.

Even though I was trying to keep my voice down, I could see someone giving me a look that said 'You are using a mobile phone, on a train, to sell shares. You are a wanker'.

The Transense sale made me a profit of about £100. But when it came to buying the just2clicks shares, the broker said, 'You do know this is the worst time to buy, don't you, mate?' 'Yeah,' I said. (Actually I didn't know that but I felt like I had a following wind and I was too excited to stop now.) 'Don't worry, I know what I'm doing,' I said. The price was 280p a share. Was I being stupid? I hope not. 'You've got to be in it to win it,' as Sally says.

21.15: Have just seen the *Nine o' Clock News* and one of the blokes from just2clicks was on. He denied that the whole thing was simply an exercise in making glorious amounts of money.

His phrase — not the reporter's — was this: 'We are not blagthecity.com.'

Friday, 18 February

Two weeks in, things are doing very nicely indeed, thank you.

It is a wonderful, warm feeling. I always suspected it would be easy, and so it has proved. My friends listen admiringly as I tell them how I've made £400 here, £200 there. It's mostly due to Autonomy, which has chugged pleasingly upwards since day one. I've made nearly ten grand on that investment alone!

My revolutionary washing machine shares are on the cycle marked 'quick profit' too: up roughly 30%, a profit of £800. And, praise the Lord, Charlton are heading for promotion, taking my investment with them. All in the garden is rosy. I am a bit of a financial genius, if truth be told, and overall, this is how my investments look:

NAME OF CO.	INITIAL STAKE	SHARE PRICE THEN	SHARE PRICE NOW	WHAT'S MY STAKE WORTH NOW, THEN?
Autonomy	£30,000	£58.55	£79.50(!)	£39,750
Charlton	£2,500	54p	59p	£2,720
MV Sports	£2,500	4p	4p	£2,500
Birchin	£2,500	12p	11p	£2,260
just2clicks	£2,500	£2.68	£2.65	£2,485
4Front	£2,500	£14.90	£15.74	£2,670
Airtel	£2,500	38p	38p	£2,500
Monotub	£2,500	£2.70	£3.62	£3,230
Monticello	£2,500	£1.10p	£1.10p	£2,500
TOTAL	£50,000			£60,615

Have called in the builders to investigate possibility of adding patio to back of house (to be paid for with fruits of my inspired investment policy)

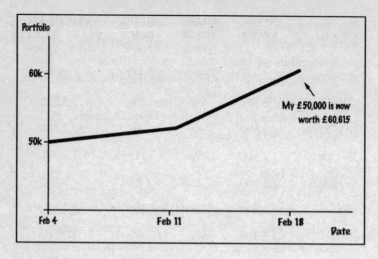

Saturday, 19 February

Spent most of the day at Sally's. Luke idolises Chelsea, so we watched the game together. I think he's going to be a journalist when he grows up: he's always asking questions. ('What do you think of Chris Sutton?' 'When you're on TV, are you doing it for real?' 'Will you really lose your house?')

I'm enjoying Sally's kids: in the way that you can when the boundaries are so clearly defined. I'm no threat, I'm not going to take Mummy away from them: I'm just the friend from down the road who comes round (a lot) to eat, watch TV and talk incessantly about stocks and shares.

I know even less about what makes relationships work than I do about the stock market, but I am at least aware of the difficulties that arise when the lines that define a relationship between a kid and an adult are blurred: an ex of mine had a seven-year-old daughter and it was all very complex.

The little girl's father, understandably, wasn't happy about me spending time with his daughter at all. The other triangle – the one that linked me, my ex and her little girl – was problematic too. No one quite knew what my role was supposed to be:

Mummy's friend, Mummy's boyfriend, or a second daddy. As a result I ended up feeling very insecure about the situation and the relationship – I knew it was happening to me and I hated it but I couldn't stop it – and the whole thing turned out to be a complete disaster.

My ex's verdict was that I was 'emotionally immature'.

Anyway: no such problems here!

Sunday, 20 February

A.M.: Well, well, well. The *Mirror*'s 'City Slickers' have been fired, and it is all over the papers and the national TV news. They have not always, it seems, been tipping from the purest of motives.

Without telling their readers, the pair have in fact been buying shares in some companies, before hyping them. Anil Bhoyrul, for instance, has been named as the owner of 10,000 shares in the restaurant group Belgo. That may explain why he's recently been encouraging his readers to 'get stuck in' to the shares in order to make 'some serious sausages and mash'. I have more than a passing interest: last month, after yet another fawning write-up on Belgo, I shelled out a few hundred quid on their shares. Nothing happened (this was in my salad-day trading days, when I was green in judgment) so I sold them later that day.

The papers are ecstatic, of course. Fleet Street loves to eat its own. Bhoyrul and his partner, James Hipwell, stand accused of being, among other things, 'spivs'. But it could get a lot more serious than this: the DTI, which prosecutes those suspected of insider dealing, have launched an investigation. It is a criminal offence under the 1986 Financial Services Act, and carries a maximum sentence of seven years in jail.

The big question is this: have the pair of them been corrupt, or stupid?

Hipwell, at least, seems to be veering towards the latter, given what his reported defence to the current charges is: he says he wasn't aware of the official rules of conduct for journalists, which forbid them having shares in companies they're writing about. Which is a bit like a policeman pleading ignorance of the law after being found smoking dope.

A lot, of course, will depend on what the DTI find out. If the Slickers were fed tips by contacts, which they accepted in good faith, and then printed (having piled in themselves) they would have been guilty of extraordinary naïvety (and breaking their professional code of conduct) but not criminal behaviour. If, however, they were aware that the information was false, then that would be a different matter. Either way, the people who suffered are the members of the public who read their column, trusted them, and ended up losing money. (Like me.) But then again, we only have ourselves to blame: if you're that gullible you deserve everything you get, I suppose. Don't believe what you read, etc. If the Slickers had been more open about things and come clean about their shareholdings, then we could at least have taken that into account, and read their tips with the required pinch of salt. And in their defence, the Slickers have got quite a few things right: a lot of their readers have undoubtedly made a lot of money from following their predictions.

Even more interesting is the role of the *Mirror*'s editor, Piers Morgan, in all this: he has kept his job, despite admitting his purchase of £20,000 worth of Viglen shares on 17 January, the day before the Slickers' lead story about the company, under the headline 'SUGAR TO JOIN NET GOLD RUSH . . .VIGLEN WEB SPIN OFF WILL SEND SHARES SOARING'. (I, you may remember, bought a few hundred quid's worth on the strength of that story myself.)

Morgan's defence is that he didn't know anything about the story until about 11.30 p.m. the night before, when he was going through the paper's first edition. This is curious, given that it's the job of an editor to read every single word of his paper before it goes to print. Morgan has now sold the shares and given the proceeds to charity. If he had been trying to make a quick killing, he argues, he would have sold them the day the story appeared, but he didn't: it was meant to be a long-term investment. What's more, he says, there had been other stories about what a good bet Viglen was, in the weeks leading up to the story in question: it was generally known that the company was looking good. In other words, the fact that he bought into Viglen big time, the day before his paper printed a story praising them to the skies, was just a coincidence. Hmmm. He is under investigation by the DTI, so it will be interesting to see what they come up with . . . and whether he'll still be in his job by the end of the year.

Even more interesting is the fact that I'm supposed to be interviewing Bhoyrul on Wednesday, for my piece on the *Tonight* programme.

P.M.: I'm no psychiatrist but the way we feel about money is, I think, determined by our upbringing. I've never really craved huge amounts of it: it's never been a motivating factor in my life. Mainly because my mother always made sure that when I needed some, I got it. Mind you, it came at a cost. She was, unfortunately, not the greatest at giving me her time, or showing me her affection. Instead she would ply me with food, and money. Love substitutes, in fact. Curiously, though, I am now finding myself increasingly excited by the money that is trickling into my coffers: but it's not the money itself that's turning me on, it's the accruing of it. This is what used to excite my mother too.

She wasn't the most conventional person in the world, I must say.

It all started going wrong when she woke up one day in the 60s and decided she was Elizabeth Taylor. Until then we'd had a reasonably conventional family unit (I was the youngest of four – three boys, one girl). My mother's new identity involved her divorcing my dad there and then. He wasn't too happy about it, apparently, but she called the shots, so that was it. It meant the end of a successful business relationship too. They ran several old people's homes in and around Epsom, in Surrey, and they were a good team: she had the creative vision, he kept an eye on the figures.

Once they parted, it all went downhill. Within five years, he'd emigrated. He'd tried turning his share of the divorce deal – two old people's homes – into hotels, but it didn't work.

She, meanwhile, in a bid to rack up an Elizabeth Taylor-style number of marriages, decided to get hitched to an ex-copper, divorce him, marry him again, and then divorce him for a second time (30 years on I think the poor bloke still doesn't know what hit him).

Like my dad, she went into hotels: and, like him, she went bust. But her journey to financial destruction was a lot more spectacular than his. Post-detective, she took up with a charming but completely feckless gay waiter called Edward, whom she'd hired to work for her. (I think she liked the challenge.) It was he, I think, who inspired her to turn her hotels into 'Gay Only' haunts. Not surprisingly it didn't go down too well with the locals. This was, after all, deeply Conservative, mid-90s Surrey. I got used to it, though: I lived in one of the hotels, so I had to. After a while the nightly gay disco, during which dozens of men wearing make-up would snog and grind their pelvises into each other, became part of my routine home life.

The local papers had a field day, of course. Outraged retired Army types queued up to denounce my mother in print ('Sergeant-Major Slams Gay Hotel Woman!') but that didn't stop her: it encouraged her. She loved the fuss.

Her next bombshell had a lot more of an effect on me, though. In 1976 she was diagnosed with cancer, but for some reason (probably because she was addicted to the publicity) she told the papers before she told me. I only found out about it when a friend at school handed me a copy of the *Epsom and Ewell Herald*, with the front-page headline 'Gay Hotel Woman Has Six Months To Live'. She was a fighter, though: thanks to a combination of drugs and chemotherapy she made it through to 1987. The trouble was, by that time I'd grown immune to her suffering: she used it as emotional blackmail. Whenever we argued (which was a lot) she would start saying, rather menacingly, 'I am a sick and dying woman and I have only six months to live.'

It may have been true but she said it so many times it ceased to have any effect on me. Once she realised that, she resorted to even more extreme tactics . . . like crawling around the floor of the kitchen in her nightdress, gasping, '. . . I am dying . . . but you want your dinner . . . and you must have your dinner, yes . . .' Looking back, I see that she just wanted a reaction, but unfortunately I couldn't give her the one she wanted.

Mind you, in the months before she did die she became very quiet and stoic. That's when I knew something really was wrong.

Monday, 21 February

P.M.: Went round to Sally's for a cup of coffee. I do like her: she is so open. Lots of people I know never admit to their neuroses, but on the basis that a problem shared is a problem solved, Sally lets you know all about hers, the moment she feels one coming to the surface. She's not bonkers, though – far from it.

She is remarkably stable, in fact: she has had to be. She survived the most horrendous divorce, and brought up two kids totally on her own.

Suddenly, just as she was stirring my coffee, she got all excited. 'Hey! Why don'you start up a website? It'd be great. Like, people can log on to see how you're doing with your investments, you could get people rilly involved.'

I couldn't face the hassle, I told her: and besides, who would be interested? I didn't understand the Internet: I was having enough problems getting to grips with the stock market as it was.

And even if I did start my own website, what would be in it for me?

Tuesday, 22 February

10.00: Maybe I was a little too hasty last night. I have just read a small paragraph in the paper about a 27-year-old from Gloucestershire called Richard Lambert, who has his own website. It's called surfworld.com, and it basically lists businesses around the world which sell surfing equipment. Richard has just sold it. For more than A Million Pounds. It was getting just 400 'hits' a day which, Sally tells me, isn't actually that many: one visitor to a site alone can be responsible for a dozen hits at a time. Hold on a minute: I could get that number of hits just by ringing up all the blokes in my cricket team!

The wheels in my mind are starting to turn.

Tuesday, 22 February

22.00: The idea of starting my own site is beginning to take me over. If it all goes according to plan I might have to change the title of this book to *How to Make Several Million from the Internet* and leave out the bit in brackets.

I was talking about it this morning with a bloke who's mortgaged his house to start up his own on-line business (hasn't everyone, darling?), and he said the three most important criteria for making a success of it were, quote, 'speed, speed and speed'.

The first thing to do once you've had your Really Great Internet Idea, he said, is to find a short, catchy name for it, and register it, pronto. An American company, Network Solutions, owns the worldwide rights to all the names in cyberspace: for around £60 you can register yours with them for two years. That is, if no one's thought of it first. In this game, names are everything. The shorter and catchier the better. Remarkably, some people have made huge fortunes by doing nothing more than simply registering a name, and then selling it: it's a bit like someone flogging a particularly sought-after car licence plate number. Except the sums involved are a *lot* bigger.

Get this: someone who had the foresight to register the name 'banks.com' sold it last year for . . . wait for it . . . seven and a half million dollars. That's almost a million dollars a letter. What's in a name, indeed.

How can those letters be worth so much? Well, I think the logic goes like this: by the end of the year 2000, in the UK alone, it's estimated that up to 20 million people will be hooked up to the Internet. A lot of them will want to use it to explore the possibility of on-line banking. This is because on-line banking is, in some ways, far more attractive than traditional high-street banking: on-line banks can offer much more attractive rates of interest, for a kick-off, because their running costs are so much lower (fewer staff, and hardly any expensive high-street buildings to maintain). A lot of would-be Internet banking customers, however, won't know where to start finding out about the whole concept: so they'll take a chance, and type in the most obvious web address they can think of. Yes, that's right. Banks.com. The owners of that address have, in theory, a licence to print money: they can charge banks a commission fee for every customer that gets signed up via the website, and they can also charge hefty amounts for advertising (for things like mortgages, financial advice, and so on). For some reason, the '.com' suffix is the Knightsbridge of cyberspace: it's by far and away the most lucrative virtual address there is.

So this evening, I went round to Sally's, fingers crossed, hoping no one had already snaffled the name I'd come up with: www.howtomakeamillion.com. We sat at her PC, and clicked a bit. Shit. It had gone. Beneath the name, there was a picture of a few men digging, accompanied by the words 'This site is under construction'. The alternatives had gone too: www.howtomake amillion.net and www.howtomakeamillion.org. Hold on: what about www.howtomakeYOURmillion.com? Click, click, click . . . woof! It's available!

We booked it there and then. (Sally did the needful with my credit card.) I kissed her on the cheek. Very nice.

OK: I may have booked the plot of land, but now I've got to build the house.

Wednesday, 23 February

A.M.: Looked into what's involved in designing, running and maintaining your own website today, but decided I just couldn't do it. I haven't got the time. So, I rang a company that specialise in it. They're called Oxygen: the ones that went up 3000% on day one of their float. They've agreed to see me . . . I'm meeting a youngish sounding woman called Emma tomorrow night.

P.M.: Interviewed Anil Bhoyrul. What he had to say off-camera was far more interesting than what he said on it: more of that in a moment. Anil and his sidekick are now working for that beacon of integrity, probity and ethics, Mohammed Al Fayed. Their column will appear every fortnight in *Punch*, the mag that Al Fayed bought back from the dead. Al Fayed also owns Fulham Football Club, which at the moment looks like a better deal than the *Punch* one: the Fulham match-day programme gets more readers.

Anil looked like a man who hadn't slept for a week: his eyes were bulging and slightly bloodshot, his skin as rough as a badger's arse. Having a conversation with him was impossible . . . every time he got a few words into a sentence his mobile would go off, and he'd start pacing around the room, saying things like, 'I want to write a book' and 'Tell him to fuck off, then'.

He was, despite what had just happened to him, still firing off share tips, like a mad gunman running amok in a shopping centre. 'Yeah, you should take a look at X, they're gonna go big this afternoon . . . Y are making an announcement on Tuesday, I know that for sure . . .'

Like most hacks, Bhoyrul was good company: I can imagine him giving value for money in the pub. He certainly gave good value before we switched the camera on for the official interview: he made several interesting allegations. Unfortunately the laws of libel mean I can't go into them here. Not at the moment anyway. All I can say is that they related to the Viglen article. The TV interview itself contained no great revelations, although he did tell us that he knew of shop assistants who'd lost five grand in a day, from day trading. (I controlled the urge to say, 'Possibly as a result of following City Slicker tips, Anil.')

Thursday, 24 February

A.M.: Went to the House of Lords to interview Baroness Young for the *Tonight* programme. She is leading the campaign to keep Clause 28: the law that stops schools 'promoting' homosexuality. Her argument is that if Clause 28 was abolished, hordes of gay activists would descend on our classrooms, trying to force obscene gay literature down kids' throats.

She showed me examples of the kind of stuff she was worried about. There was a booklet from the 80s, about a little girl with two gay parents, called *Jenny Lives with Eric and Martin*. This appalled her, you could tell: she held it at arm's length as she leafed through it, like a smelly piece of fish.

During the interview I asked her if she was worried that children might 'catch' homosexuality if they were exposed to this kind of thing.

'Yes, absolutely,' she said.

Normally, current affairs reporters on TV aren't allowed to have opinions on the subjects they cover. Or at least they're not allowed to express them in their reports. On *Tonight*, though, we've bent those unwritten rules a little: Michael Nicholson, a grey-haired buffer in a V-necked jumper whose name never appears in print without the words 'veteran reporter' next to it, can regularly be seen expressing moral outrage about something or other (e.g. the treatment of Kurds in Turkey).

For some people, this is sacrilege: current affairs is sacred, they argue, the reporter is there to report, not opine. I disagree: how can you expect someone not to have an opinion on something as powerful as the death of a child? It also makes for better and more compelling TV, and, hopefully, bigger audiences. People in telly always get slagged off by the snotty, sneery commentators for 'chasing ratings', but I think that's bollocks: what's wrong with wanting the programmes you do to be watched by as many people as possible?

But on a sensitive issue like this Jeff the editor told me, I had to tread mega carefully: no opinions. If you were perceived to be even slightly bending over backwards to accommodate the gays, so to speak, the Baroness Youngs and the Angries from Tunbridge Wells of this world would go bonkers. Likewise, if you took up a family-values-Baroness-Young-*Daily Mail* position, the café-latte-quaffing *Guardian*-reading Islington crowd would start complaining.

P.M.: Saw Emma from Oxygen. She is based in a small office on an industrial estate in Kilburn in North London. She is in her late 20s, dark, posh, and quite intense. She's reasonably sexy, in a cerebral kind of way: the sort of woman you find more attractive at the end of a long conversation than you did at the beginning. The moment we first met, the appalling sexist pig in me thought, Oh God, she's just a kid, what does she know, but it became very clear, very quickly, that she knew her cyber onions big time.

I told her my plans: it was obvious, from the little I'd read about websites, that the key thing was to make them 'sticky': i.e. sticky enough for people to hang around for as long as possible on the site. That way they're more likely to a) buy something or b) take notice of the adverts. Apparently if someone stays with you for 10 minutes you're doing well.

Just posting up the details of my portfolio in cyberspace, I realised, wouldn't detain punters for long, so I was planning to have two other features, the first being 'The Early Bird'. This, I explained to Emma, would be a round-up of all the financial pages from all nine of the national newspapers (excluding the *Daily Star*). Particular attention would be paid to all the share tips: dead useful for anyone thinking of doing what I was doing (albeit in less dramatic fashion). Apparently someone from Bolton has already done this, and got himself a sizable audience, but he had to give up. He lived so far out in the sticks he couldn't get all the papers delivered in time. I, however, have lined up my mate Dave, an unemployed screenwriter from North London, to cycle to King's Cross station every night to pick up all the papers, and have them written up by 3 a.m. I'm giving him pocket money and 1% of the company. So if it gets sold for a million, he gets 10k.

I loved the sensation of offering him a slice of the company, it made me feel like a real entrepreneur: but this is the way it's working for real, too. In the City at the moment, new hi-tech outfits coming to the market are getting big law firms to do hundreds of thousands of pounds' worth of paperwork, not for cash, but for shares – i.e. a slice of what the company might be worth in the future.

The second feature, I told Emma, would be a weekly share tip, written (apparently) by a cartoon character called Hugo The Man In The Know. Virtual (i.e. cyber) people clearly have great poten- tial: Sally's son really fancies Lara Croft, and I read the other day that the rights to Ananova, a sexy virtual newscaster, have been sold for several million quid. I saw Hugo, I told Emma, as a cross between Captain Mainwaring out of *Dad's Army* and one of those small, black-suited and bowler-hatted Homepride Flour men.

The bloke I've lined up to write that, coincidentally, looks not unlike a human version of the character I have in mind. (Just take away the bowler hat and add a big woolly cardigan.) His name is Robin, the producer of a financial show on Sky TV. He's been here before: 12 months ago, he was offered a job with a new financial website, and a 10% stake in it. He turned it down because the salary wasn't high enough. Bad move. Three months ago, the site was bought out for £9,000,000. If he'd said yes, he'd have made £900,000.

I offered him a nominal fee for each article and 2% of my company and he accepted like a flash.

So what did Emma think?

'Yeah, wicked. We'll do it for you.' She said Oxygen would do all the hassley, technical stuff for me if I gave them 5% of the company.

Fine, I said. Deal!

As I left she asked me which companies I reckoned were good investment bets. I couldn't bear to give her any tips, I said, in case they went wrong.

Friday, 25 February

On the way up to Manchester this morning I read about the UK's top ten richest cyberkids. There, at number six, was Emma. Worth nine million, it said. Hold on. Only last night she was asking me for share tips and here she is, in the papers, supposedly worth £9 million. What does she want share tips for? Strange days we're living in.

The portfolio, meanwhile, is blooming. Autonomy is going great guns: it's earned me more than £10,000 since I bought it. On the downside, just2clicks has bombed: down almost 30% in

DIGGING DEEPER | 77

a week. I've lost more than £600 on it. I should have listened to the bloke who warned me against buying shares on the first day of a public flotation. That City saying ('In every market there's a fool. If you don't know who the fool is, it's probably you') springs to mind – again.

Anyway, here's how things look:

NAME OF CO.	INITIAL STAKE	SHARE PRICE THEN	SHARE PRICE NOW	WHAT'S MY STAKE WORTH NOW, THEN?
Autonomy	£30,000	£58.55	£81.75	£40,875
Charlton	£2,500	54p	59p	£2,720
MV Sport	£2,500	4p	3.75p	£2,250
Birchin	£2,500	12p	11p	£2,260
just2clicks	£2,500	£2.68	£1.70	£1,820
4Front	£2,500	£14.90	£15.95	£2,710
Airtel	£2,500	38p	39.5p	£2,560
Monotub	£2,500	£2.70	£3.59	£3,200
Monticello	£2,500	£1.10	£1.02	£2,270
TOTAL	£50,000			£60,670

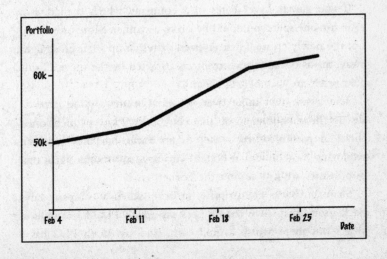

Monday, 28 February

There is a little table on one of the financial websites I use which lists the day's biggest movers and shakers – in both directions. Most of the time, if a company's share price rises or falls 5%, it will get a mention. This morning I almost fell out of my tree: within minutes of the market opening, a company's share price had fallen from roughly £30 to £6: a fall of more than 80%!

I know buying on the dips isn't always a good idea, but the company concerned was a strong, healthy one, with good prospects . . . this was a gilt-edged buying opportunity if ever there was one.

On closer inspection, however, it turned out things weren't quite what they seemed: the company had done something called 'A Four-For-One Split'. This means, as you might have already guessed, that they'd split each one of their shares into four. The reason for this is simple: if the price of an individual share is too high, e.g. £1000, it will deter smaller investors. They might only want to invest £500 a time. If, however, that firm split each of their shares into four, they would then cost only £250: far more affordable.

If you *already* have shares in a company which then does a four-for-one split, you could be on to a winner. More often than not the newly created quarter-sized shares go up a fair bit straight away: this is because new investors, attracted by the more afford-able price, are clambering aboard.

The lesson isn't quite over yet: now seems a good time to discuss the phenomenon of 'share buybacks'. I know I mentioned them in passing when I met Adam Faith, but they're worth exploring more as they're (often) an important smoke signal that good times are just around the corner.

Share buybacks are, surprise, surprise, when a company buys back some of its own shares. Let's say Akash PLC has a million shares out there, worth a quid each. And say Akash PLC has a load of spare dosh, and thinks their prospects are good. They might then use that dosh to buy back 900,000 of their shares, for £900,000, knowing that when things do improve, they can sell them for a lot more. This means there are now only 100,000 shares remaining on the market. Those 100,000 shares will now be more valuable: simply because there are a lot less of them on the market than there were. People will want to buy them, and once they do, they go up in price. So: when you read about directors buying back their own shares, it's normally quite a healthy sign: they might well know something good that you don't. You might want to buy!

Here endeth the lesson.

Tuesday, 29 February

One of the great skills you need as an investor is the ability to read through, and understand, a prospectus. Any firm wanting to offer shares to the public will have one. In fact, at the moment anyone who runs a business printing the things must be coining it: it's not unusual for a new company to send out 100,000 (several times the circulation of *Punch*) to would-be investors.

I know they're even more boring than watching an episode of *Panorama*. But they are important, as they're the only clues we get as to whether the firm is a good bet or not. The prospectus will, of course, make out that the company is but one small step away from taking over the world, and all they need is your money to help them do it.

But you shouldn't fall for that: what you're supposed to do, apparently, is check out the backgrounds of the main players in the firm (there will be a page devoted to their CVs). Have they got relevant experience? Have they worked for well-known companies? Also, look at the figures. (Hard, I know: reading a balance sheet doesn't come naturally to most of us.) Is the company making a profit? Is it making any money at all? Is it ever likely to? How big is the market it's going into? How many competitors is it likely to have? What makes this company more likely to succeed than the rest of them?

There can be no definitive answers to these questions, of course, but you'll be less likely to lose your dosh if you at least try to answer some of them.

The hardest task of all, especially when it comes to hi-tech firms, is working out what the company actually does. It's all very well being told that Wizzbang PLC, for example, make a brand-new type of fibre optic cable wire, but where does that leave you?

An example: this morning I read a prospectus for a company who make 'software applications that deal with knowledge and collaboration . . . rather than the traditional data transaction systems currently used such as enterprise resource planning . . .' What?

The trouble is, at the moment a lot of people don't really care what's in a prospectus, as long as it's got the magic terms '.com' and 'Internet' in it. Right now, so many people are applying for shares in new companies you could print a prospectus for one called 'sendusyourmoney.com' and cheques would be pouring in the next day.

Come to think of it, that's pretty much what a prospectus I read this morning is doing. The firm concerned doesn't actually make anything, they just want to invest in other companies that do: in fact, says the blurb, they may even invest in other companies *like themselves*.

This last bit is astonishing, when you think about it.

In the old days, as far as I can tell, you, the DIY punter, invested directly in a company that actually did something. Now, you're being asked to invest in companies that do nothing, apart from invest in other companies.

In fact you might well end up investing in a company which does nothing but invest in other companies which do nothing apart from investing in other companies which do nothing but . . . and so on.

In the end there could be millions of these so-called 'Internet incubator' companies, who will do nothing but invest your money in each other. Then, presumably, the moment they can cash in, they will.

And walk off with (what's left of) your money.

What gave the game away in the prospectus I read this morning was the sheer shamelessness of the entire thing: there was a badly printed letter that came with it, which said, effectively, 'Please send your cheques to the above address. We work on the basis that it's first come first served' – i.e. send us as much of your money as possible now, or you might not get any shares. The address to send the cheques to was a private house, in North London. The whole thing smacked of a not very well disguised pyramid selling operation.

I may be stupid but I'm not that stupid.

Thursday, 2 March

11.00: Checked the Autonomy Beard Corporation price. It's the same it's been all week: roughly £90. I'm not complaining: I bought thirty grand's worth when it was £60 so I've made a paper profit of 10k in less than a month. I am going to do some exercise.

12.30: Blimey. Just checked it again before going into work. It's now £100. Hmmmm. That means I'm almost 5k richer than I was before I got on my exercise bike 90 minutes ago.

Mustn't get too excited, though. Two weeks ago there was a massive rise, followed almost immediately by a substantial fall: three steps forward, one step back.

13.30: There is slightly more excitement at work than usual. This is because Martin 'Bish-Bosh' Bashir has done an exclusive interview with Jeffrey Archer for tonight's programme. A line from a pop song – 'what goes up, must come down' – keeps blaring, again and again, out of the editing room next to our main office where he's putting the report together.

Every so often there is raucous laughter, punctuated by the sight of Bish–Bosh looking stern and tense, striding in and out of the room.

For some reason, whenever you ask Martin how it's going he feels unable to give you a straight answer: he prefers rugby metaphors.

'We're 10–0 up. What we've got to do now is put a high ball in their twenty-two and *bang!* hit them hard just as they catch the ball.'

He punched his fist into his palm for effect on the 'bang'.

I tried to work out what he meant but, despite being a rugby fan, I couldn't. However, my guess is that things are going well, as I just saw Jeff, The Editor Who Doesn't Smile Much, Especially On Programme Day, smiling. I'm going home.

18.00: Ohfuckme. I don't believe what I'm seeing. There is a figure in front of me that bears no relation to the one I saw at lunch-time. The share price at which the Beard Corporation closed was £120: I got in at £60. I have made 30k in four weeks, 20k in one day. I need to tell someone.

18.30: Sally laughed. 'Congratulations. You're hooked.'

Less hooked, more about to – spontaneously – combust. I have made £20,000 in a day. At this rate I will be a millionaire in 50 days. I am now striding around my front room, smoking a Silk Cut Ultra, asking her the same thing over and over again. Should I sell? Often, if a share skyrockets, it falls soon after.

'What goes up, must come down' in fact.

This is because, at perceived high points, lots of people start selling some, but not all, of their shares, so they can make a few quid in profit on their original investments. At that point, because there are more sellers than buyers, according to the basic laws of supply and demand, the price falls.

Hmmmm. If I cash in all my chips first thing tomorrow, before it starts to slide back, I'll have £60,000 of real money – not just a paper profit – in my bank account. When – if? – it slips a bit, to £110, say, I could reinvest the lot.

That way, if it goes up again, I'll be making money on it twice. Then again, if I sell, and – eek – the share price carries on going up from £120, to, say, £140, I'll have to hop back on board the speeding bus. And the price of having missed out on that part of the journey will be £10,000 in lost profits.

18.40: Just checked the share price again to make sure. Still £120. Fuckfuckfuck. What am I going to do? I've bought a juicy steak from Marks and Spencer on the way home from work, but for once in my life I'm really not hungry. Whoever said adrenaline suppresses your appetite was right.

23.00: Have just watched Martin's interview with Lord Archer. Compelling and surreal. It started with shots of Archer doing knee flexes in the gym, to the sounds of 'what goes up, must come down'. He kept producing his made-for-TV smile and saying things like 'I am stupid' and 'Mary is a very remarkable woman'.

It ended with him on-stage, in the spotlight, reciting lines from a play he'd written. And – I don't think he's joking – he intends to take the lead role himself.

I will decide what to do tomorrow morning after a night's not sleeping.

Friday, 3 March
08.10: A sensible compromise. I sold half my shares. This means a profit – a real cash one – of £30,000 is heading for my NatWest bank account. This is what is called 'Top Slicing', i.e. creaming off profits, but leaving a fair number of your shares still in there, 'working for you'.

Or, as Sally keeps saying, 'You gotta be in it to win it, Jonathan.'
09.00: Rang Richard (Normal). Reminded him what he said

when I told him to buy Autonomy last month ('I think it's peaked'). He laughed. A bit.

Read the papers. Autonomy are on the front page of the *FT!* The headline says, 'INVESTORS GO WILD OVER CAMBRIDGE GROUP'S WEB FILTER'. And on the financial pages of the *Daily Mail* . . . there is a picture of Mike Lynch, perched next to a computer, looking surprisingly unenthusiastic but, reassuringly, fully bearded. In fact the beard looks a lot more bushy than normal: maybe it's coming out in sympathy with the share price. Unlike the company, though, it hasn't doubled in a month. More like 25%. The *Mail* proclaimed: 'AUTONOMY SHARES UP 52% AND IT LOOKS LIKE A PATTERN'.

The reason for Miracle Thursday, it turns out, is that Lynchy has signed contracts with 50 big computer manufacturers: every time they make a new computer, they will bung his invention in it.

I don't know if there was a company around at the birth of the motor car which invented and copyrighted the steering wheel; but if there was, through judgment instinct/luck, I think I may have bought into the modern-day equivalent. In a way it's even better than that: Lynchy has signed royalty agreements with the companies that use his product: so not only does he get paid for each steering wheel, he gets money from the petrol company, every time someone fills up their tank.

And even if I'm wrong £30,000 in cash is heading for my bank account anyway.

I now feel much calmer than I did 15 minutes ago. I will spend the day working from home and rehearsing for Surf 'n' Turf's next gig, a wedding in Devon tomorrow. Unfortunately the day has a fishing theme, and so the bride's parents want us all to dress up as fishermen.

18.00: As it happens, Autonomy Beard have kept on growing. They closed at £130. I still have £30,000 in there so I'm still getting the benefit — but not as much as if I'd kept the whole lot in. Who cares. I've done OK.

Saturday, 4 March

Read a scary article on the way down to Devon. There's no doubt the bubble is going to burst: it's not a case of if, but when. Will I get out in time? It pointed out that in America, one small company set up to trade specialised steel products over the Internet is now already worth as much as the entire steel industry. Oh dear. That can't be right. I feel like I'm in a ship full of free cash that's slowly sinking: should I swim for shore now with a huge armful, or carry on stuffing my swagbags and risk drowning and losing the whole lot? Yesterday, at least, I sent some on to dry land in a dinghy. But I've still got plenty left in: and I intend to buy more with the profits I've made. I reckon there's some way to go, though: more and more people – private investors – want to join the fun, so there's an ever increasing amount of dosh coming to the market.

Matt, the guitarist in Surf 'n' Turf, for example.

As I write this, he is driving us down to the West Country wedding gig. He has the investing habits of an old woman, and he wants to go on-line. He has a couple of grand to play with. And there are up to three million more like him waiting in the wings. And that's just in the UK.

I feel OK about ignoring all the prophets of doom who keep on saying 'Beware the crash is nigh – hi-tech stocks are ludicrously overvalued' because, it seems to me, they're not distinguishing between the different types of hi-tech company: ones like Autonomy, who have a proper, proven product, which works, and sells round the world, and ones like Lastminute. com, who don't. They just provide a service: and it's a service a lot of other companies provide.

Hmmmm. I hope our gig works out well tonight: I accidentally had seven pints of extra-strong lager before our last one and (I'm told) made rather a huge and horrible dent in our usually polished sound. This has been a source of great distress to me and I want to make it up to the rest of the band tonight by being as uncrap as possible.

Sunday, 5 March

A.M.: Phew! We went down well. Although it did feel a little undignified playing in a hayloft in a big barn, dressed in a yellow sou–wester, sailor's hat, neckerchief and fisherman's smock. Our version of 'Walking On Sunshine' was a thing of joy and beauty. Music is the best. Am going to Sally's for dinner.

Oh, and by the way, here is the (very pleasing) state of play:

NAME OF CO.	INITIAL STAKE	SHARE PRICE THEN	SHARE PRICE NOW	WHAT'S MY STAKE WORTH NOW, THEN?
Autonomy	£30,000	£58.55p	£121	£60,250
Charlton	£2,500	54p	59p	£2,270
MV Sports	£2,500	4p	3.75p	£2,250
Birchin	£2,500	12p	15p	£3,250
just2clicks	£2,500	£2.68	£1.68	£1,795
Airtel	£2,500	38p	39p	£2,530
Monotub	£2,500	£2.70p	£3.52	£3,110
Monticello	£2,500	£1.10p	95p	£2,125
4Front	£2,500	£14.90	£16.10	£2,790
TOTAL	£50,000			£80,370

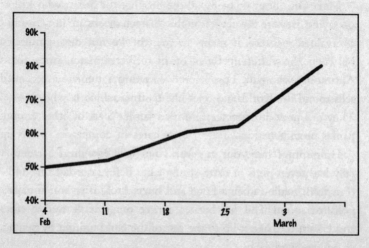

Yours truly basking contentedly in window, smoking a fag & feeling remarkably pleased with myself (Ok & just a bit smug too)

Patio builders on way back to HQ: who needs one, when you'll soon be moving to a million pound house with full amenities already built (including studio for 'Surf 'n' Turf' & putting green & bunker in back garden)

Tuesday, 7 March

I may have started a trend. The City Slickers have announced in *Punch* that they too are aiming to make a million by the end of the year, via the stock market. Unlike me, however, they are not mortgaging their houses but getting the mag's owner, Mohamed al Fayed – yes, him again – to bankroll them. He is giving them 100k to play with. They are also writing a book, to be called *How to Make Your Million in the City*. It shouldn't be a long one: I can sum it up for them in 28 words. 'Start a share tipping column in a national paper. Buy shares in companies. Whip up their prospects in your column. Then sell. But, unlike us, don't get caught.'

This could be a coincidence, but when I told Bhoyrul – possibly unwisely – what I was doing during our interview the other week, his eyes lit up. They have actually mentioned me, in passing, in their column: but only to say that I've mortgaged my house. No mention of the million-pound target, or the book. And, displaying their now legendary reputation for accuracy and integrity, they have 1) spelt my name wrong, 2) got the name of the show I work for (*Tonight with Trevor McDonald*) wrong, and 3) failed to say where they appear to have got their inspiration from.

I'm not too bothered, though.

Wednesday, 8 March
In all the serious relationships I've had with women (seven) there has always been a moment – a tangible, memorable one – when I realised that the genie was out of the bottle, and that from then on, no matter what happened, I would fall in love with them. The actual events that triggered the realisation were pretty mundane: the last time was more than three years ago, when a friend of mine got into a taxi, just after we'd said goodbye to each other, on the Putney Bridge Road. I don't know how or why it happened: pre-taxi, we were friends. Post-taxi, everything changed.

I think something may have happened again. This time it's been set off by vegetables. Sally was chopping them in her kitchen when I found myself looking at her, and thinking how quintessentially lovely she was. Then I realised I'd been looking at her for much longer than was strictly necessary. Now I'm worried. Do I say anything? Would it ruin everything? Maybe I'm imagining it. I will sleep on it.

Thursday, 9 March
No, I'm not imagining it. I know because I woke up this morning thinking about her: the acid test. Oh God. What am I going to do?

Friday, 10 March

I'm not quite as obsessed with my portfolio as I was – it's going so well there doesn't seem much to worry about (see below). Just over a month in and I've made more than 30k. My original investment is now worth more than £83,000. If I keep this monthly rate of increase up I will be a millionaire in less than four months! In which case I will have to speak to Hodder's, the publishers of this book, about bringing the publication date forward.

So far it's proving almost disappointingly easy: all I've done is pick a few shares, sit back, and watch the money roll in. Even the ones I picked at random, with no research at all, like 4Front – because I liked the name – have done the business for me.

All I have to do next is to decide what to do with my lovely little cash pile of £30,000 which came my way last week, and which is now nestling in a specially created bank account at the Clapham Junction branch of the NatWest:

◇ **NatWest**   Current Plus Account

Branch details	Summary	9 Feb 2000 to 14 Mar 2000 Sheet 2
CLAPHAM JUNCTION 66-68 ST JOHN'S ROAD CLAPHAM JUNCTION LONDON SW11 1PB	Previous balance	£0.00
0845 605 16 05	Taken out	£0.00
	Paid in	£30,145.92
	New balance	£30,145.92

MR J J MAITLAND

LONDON

YOU BETTER BELIEVE IT

I'm going to reinvest it all: but not yet. I need to find some likely targets.

NAME OF CO.	INITIAL STAKE	SHARE PRICE THEN	SHARE PRICE NOW	WHAT'S MY STAKE WORTH NOW, THEN?
Autonomy	£30,000	£58.55	£126.50	£62,800
				(including cash in bank)
Charlton	£2,500	54p	62p	£2,670
MV Sports	£2,500	4p	2.75p	£1,670
Birchin	£2,500	12p	12p	£2,500
just2clicks	£2,500	£2.68	£1.70	£1,805
Airtel	£2,500	38p	42p	£2,725
Monotub	£2,500	£2.70	£4.10	£3,660
Monticello	£2,500	£1.10	90p	£2,020
4Front	£2,500	£14.90	£19.75	£3,160
TOTAL	£50,000			£83,010

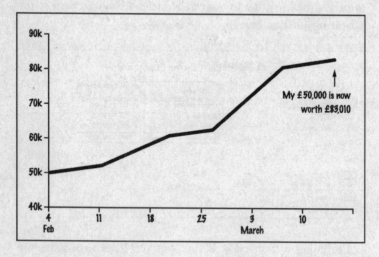

On the personal front I have started behaving differently with Sally, doing all those things you do when you know you're going down fast, like 1) throwing out loads of (I hope) subtle compliments, 2) offering to do lots of out-of-character things like moving furniture, 3) taking more care over my appearance and 4) generally playing the 'nice guy' card.

I don't think she's noticed. But it feels good feeling like this anyway.

Wednesday, 15 March

Martha Lane Fox is all over the papers like a rash. Yesterday Lastminute floated on the stock market and now it's 'worth' £700 million apparently. Mind you, it was worth £600 million before lunch and £800 million after. Now I know what 'volatile' means. It seems glaringly obvious to me that a year from now the company will be worth less than half of that: if I'm wrong I'll run up and down the road I live in naked, with a copy of the *FT*, screaming, 'Forgive me, Martha, I was wrong'. The problem is simple: in my opinion, the company isn't very good. I find the website hard to use and it doesn't save you that much money anyway. Oh yes: and lots of other companies are doing the same thing. And it doesn't make a profit. Not yet anyway. In fact the Akash, my local curry house, looks a better investment: as this table shows:

NAME OF COMPANY	LASTMINUTE.COM	AKASH
NUMBER OF VISITORS TO SITE IN THREE MONTHS UP TO DECEMBER 1999	655,000	6,000
% OF THOSE VISITORS WHO ACTUALLY BOUGHT SOMETHING	5%	100%
% OF THOSE VISITORS WHO WILL TURN INTO LOYAL REGULAR CUSTOMERS	UNKNOWN	85%

TURNOVER IN THREE MONTHS UP TO DECEMBER 1999	£300,000	£60,000
PROFIT	NONE (LOSING SEVERAL MILLION A YEAR)	£30,000
BEARD FACTOR	NEGLIGIBLE	COPIOUS: TONY THE OWNER LOOKS LIKE HE'S GOT A GUARDS-MAN'S HAT UNDER HIS CHIN
CHANCES OF GETTING WHAT YOU WANT, E.G. ONION BHAJEE OR CHEAP FLIGHT	UNCERTAIN	NO PROBLEM (BHAJEES VERY CRISP AND SERVED WITHIN SECONDS)
CURRENT STOCK MARKET VALUE	£800 MILLION	NIL

Well? What do you think? Which company would you rather invest in?

Thursday, 16 March

A.M.: No danger of me disrobing in the near future. Lastminute dot bomb has been sinking slowly and inexorably throughout the day and is now worth roughly £100 million less than it was yesterday. It could be a long way down.

Some commentators are drawing parallels between Martha Lane Fox and Sophie Mirman, an entrepreneur who was (briefly) all the rage in the 80s. Like Martha, Sophie was female, attractive, in the papers a lot, and had a Big Idea that would Change

The Face Of The High Street. Sophie's was niche marketing. Her 'Sock Shop' chain did rather well for a bit, and at one stage it seemed that a string of highly profitable niche outlets would follow: Tie Shop, Hat Shop, etc. But then things started going wrong. She tried to expand too quickly and it all came crashing down. Eventually the administrators were called in and the company was bought out. Lord knows if the same thing will happen to Martha, but if I was her I'd be a bit worried. I have rung her PR company and asked for an interview to see what she thinks about it all but they have fobbed me off. I'll let the dust settle and try again later.

Tonight I'm going to Sally's for dinner. I'm finding it harder and harder not to tell her how I feel. I keep thinking of the Cat Stevens song that goes 'Can't keep it in, I can't keep it in and I gotta let it out'. It's very much affecting the way I am with her and I'm surprised she hasn't noticed. I've tried transmitting messages through my eyes when I talk to her which say 'I'm finding you deeply attractive, please tell me you feel the same so I won't have to run the risk of telling you first and getting rejected', but it doesn't seem to work. But I have a plan. A form of words.

Midnight: Just got home and have had a few. We talked for a bit in the kitchen and then went and sat on the sofa. She sat near me. Not next to me, though. There was a gap in the conversation. I had my line ready. But then she started talking about something else just as I was throwing the ball up in the air and getting ready to serve. Then another gap. I said it. 'Do you . . . think there's – erm – any danger of this relationship going on to another level?' Not bad, I thought. I'm not saying 'Go out with me' so she can't say 'No'. But I knew straight away it wasn't looking good. It was the way she smiled. It wasn't a happy smile but a resigned, slightly pitying one. She didn't want to ruin our friendship, she said. That was what it all boiled down to. Or maybe she just didn't fancy me and didn't want to hurt my feelings. Whatever: after a few minutes I reckoned a dignified retreat was the best option. Lick my wounds at home. As I opened the door to leave she hugged me and kissed me on the cheek. I feel a bit crap. Maybe she'll see the error of her ways in the morning.

Friday, 17 March

11.30: No she won't. Earlier I got a long e-mail from her. She wants things to stay as they are . . . and she couldn't bear it if things didn't work out. Hmm. That last bit gives me slight hope, though: at least she's entertained the prospect of us going out. Thirty minutes ago she actually came round to do some computer stuff and it was all a bit awkward. I consciously tried not to look at her and we didn't say a thing about last night, or her e-mail. Funny: she could talk about all those intimate things via cyberspace, but not face to face. The Internet is good for taking the awkwardness out of intimacy.

The big problem now is this book: until last week, and the Moment When I Watched Her Chop Vegetables, she had been reading every word. I couldn't bear to show her what I've written now. I'll just have to make excuses.

23.00: I am depressed. I am trying to learn the bass line of 'Bohemian Rhapsody' by Queen, which means playing the thing over and over again. I am depressed a) because of Sally and b) because the song reminds me of being stuck in my study at boarding school, aged 16, at weekends, when all my day-boy pals were out on the town, losing their virginity. But I must carry on: I'm doing a pilot programme for a TV show next week, which involves me and my mate Rajan inviting celebs round to 'our flat' for a musical jam session. The celeb is Tara Palmer-Tomkinson, who plays piano, and this is the song she wants to play with us. It's not exactly easy. And God knows what we'll sound like.

And I still don't know how to play it. (Sally, not 'Bohemian Rhapsody', that is.)

I was supposed to be taking her out for dinner tomorrow and she's throwing a party for me at her place on the 27th, as it's my birthday. I feel like calling both events off.

Great.

She's the first person I've felt able to fall for in years and it's not reciprocated.

I hope I feel better tomorrow.

Saturday, 18 March

I don't. I did laugh for the first time in 72 hours this morning, though: I told my mate Richard ('It's peaked') about Sally's e-mail and he said, 'So she sent you a "DearJohn@" letter, then.' I can't face going out with her tonight, so I've made an excuse about having to work.

How can I pretend to be cool and fun when all I want to do is talk about how much I want to go out with her? The party feels like it's over. On both counts.

My emotional stock market graph has fallen 25% in three days. The real thing has too: Internet stocks have taken a hell of a rogering in the same period and my portfolio is down by about 5k. In fact it's got so bad all the papers are saying this is it, the bubble is bursting.

Apparently Big Cheeses at The Government Treasury Department have been having High-Level Talks to discuss Concerns that the mad rush into overvalued Internet stocks might seriously affect the economy! Me and my lemmings could be in danger of blowing up the monetary national grid!

I'm not too worried, though: I have a goodly proportion of my 30k Autonomy Beard profits nestling snugly in my bank account, and now is the time to Keep The Faith/Sit On My Hands/Take A Long-Term View/Not Panic, etc. Everyone seems to be buying back into all the old faithful companies like Diageo (the makers of Guinness) and Hanson, but I want explosive growth and I can't see it coming from brewers and supermarkets.

What is worrying me is the lack of news from the Oxygen lot; they said they'd send the website design to me two days ago and I haven't heard a thing. It's got to be up, running and functional in eight days.

I also need publicity for it, badly: if no one knows about it no one will log on and I won't be able to sell it for several trillion. For fledgling dotcoms like mine, publicity is oxygen. I can't pay for any advertising, as a decent TV and poster campaign would cost millions. And it would be wasted millions anyway. There are so many dotcom adverts at the moment that it's impossible to tell them apart. What's more, most of them are shite: they're so busy being up-their-own-arse clever, they don't actually do what they're supposed to: i.e. tell you what the company being advertised actually *does*.

There was one very expensive-looking one the other day, for a company called 'boo'. It featured lots of attractive young people playing baseball. What's boo for, though? I still dunno. The people making these adverts seem to forget that the Net is still very new and very scary for a lot of people and it all needs explaining in words of one syllable.

I have a plan, though: as a journalist, if I can persuade newspaper editors that I've come up with a good enough story, they'll print it. And surely mortgaging your house to play the stock market and then making more than £30,000 in your first month is a pretty good story?

I'm going to make a few calls.

Sunday, 19 March

Midnight: smoking a Silk Cut Ultra listening to 'The Boys Are Back In Town' by Thin Lizzy. You might think it's naff, but to me it is, as my father used to say, 'Proper music played by professionals'. I had forgotten how good this song was, and how it made me feel. I may suggest it as an addition to the Surf 'n' Turf canon, but I'm sure it'll get knocked back. The reason for Thin Lizzy is that I've just seen them play live at the Worcester Park Tavern in Surrey. Or rather their tribute band, Dizzy Lizzy. They were great. ('They really keep music alive,' said Richard. Quite profound if you think about it.) I am a bit out of it and felt the need to hear the real thing as soon as I got through the door. When Dizzy Lizzy played 'Still In Love With You' I came over all nostalgic/sentimental about the time I wrote out the song's entire lyrics and sent them to my first ever proper girlfriend when she was working as a waitress in the South of France. We were both 18.

'I think I'll go to pieces if I don't find something else to do, the sadness it never ceases, oh, I'm still in love with you . . .' was how it began. That summer I hitch-hiked out to see her. When I got there I discovered that soon after the receipt of aforementioned lyrics she had shagged a French waiter.

Which was a bit uncalled for.

Anyway, I feel a bit better. Having a good time has helped me come to terms with the Sally thing. I actually managed to stop thinking about it for a couple of hours, and now that I'm pissed and looking at it afresh, the course I must take seems clearer. I was tempted to stop seeing her as much, as being confronted all the time by something that I couldn't have was getting me down. But why stop being friends with her just because she doesn't want to go out with me? That would be throwing the baby, and indeed the whole bath, out with the bath water. I am going to be mature and put it to the back of my mind.

I have a big week coming up: I still haven't seen the website design but Carl the Stubborn Northerner from Oxygen says he'll e-mail it to me first thing Monday. There will be one problem.

I want music on it. He doesn't. He says it puts people off. I don't care. I just think it would be great, and different.

I asked him if there was any research that showed that people's all-important 'stickiness' factor on websites was lessened by music.

He said, 'Yes. Carl research.'

I've also got to make sure the paper round-up is accurate, literate, comprehensive and brief, and find people to advertise. How I do that, I haven't a clue.

Not to mention the technical nightmares. Who counts the clicks?

Mind you, I have sown seeds in the minds of editors at the Media *Guardian* and the *Independent*. They are 'quite' interested in me writing a piece for them, but there's no guarantee they'll publish it.

Monday, 20 March

13.00: Woof! I've just got my first advertiser for the website! I managed to fit in a quick round of golf before work this morning and one of the blokes I was playing with was Simon Rhodes, the marketing director of PPP, the private healthcare company. When I told him what I was up to, he said, 'That's brilliant. We should take an advert out on it.' A couple of phone calls later – deal done.

They're going to put their logo up on the site, with the slogan 'What is wealth without health?' underneath. It stays there for three months, and I get five grand. Five thousand pounds!

I just hope I can get the publicity in the papers that I told him I could.

14.00: That shouldn't be a problem: someone just rang and told me I'm in the *Guardian* today. There is a small paragraph in their gossip column: 'Jonathan Maitland, boyish *Tonight* reporter and former *Watchdog* mainstay, has a new project. He's remortgaged his house for £50,000 and plans to make himself a millionaire within a year, day trading on the Internet. He's well on his way, having increased his lump sum to £84,000 by the end of the first month. The project is creating so much interest that publishers Hodder and Stoughton have paid £15,000 for a book. Green with envy? Not us.'

Boyish? I'm 38.

15.00: Goodnessgoodnessgraciousme. The BBC have been on the blower and want to make a documentary about me. The phone is now ringing approx. every five minutes. And the website design still hasn't arrived.

The trouble is, the articles I'm writing for the papers are pencilled in for a week today, and I'm aiming to (subtly) plug the site big time. If it's not up and running the whole thing will be a waste of time: thousands of people could be logging on to something that isn't there.

15.30: Sally has just popped round. She is worried about someone nicking my name and exploiting it on the Internet. It might sound ridiculous but she has a point: I read an article in the *Mail on Sunday* yesterday which said that so-called 'cyber-squatters' are registering well-known names and then trying to sell them back to the people involved for thousands of pounds. It's happened to Zoe Ball already: someone's named a website after her and put mocked-up porno pictures of her on it. Talk about Invasion Of The Bodysnatchers . . . this is the Invasion Of The Identity Snatchers.

The thing is, I'm a D-grade celeb: who on earth would want to nick my name? But Sally reckons it's worth insuring against, just in case this thing takes off and I become a grade C or even B. All you do is pay someone out there £75 and you own your own name. Seems a bit unnecessary to me, but there we go.

16.00: Whew! The front page of the site has arrived, via e-mail.

This is what they've sent me:

Exciting, or what! I am now a publishing magnate! (Or at least I will be when the thing gets posted up in cyberspace.)

Tuesday, 21 March

22.00: Just been to the Akash. Spent the day filming with Tara P-T. We were worried she wouldn't enter into the spirit of it all but we needn't have been: after three minutes she leaped up from her piano stool and screamed, 'Eau Gord, this is suuuuch fun!'

She was a lot thinner than I imagined she'd be.

Our version of 'Bohemian Rhapsody' won't be troubling the pop chart compilers: Tara plonked out the piano part (painfully) with one finger while the rest of us provided a backing track of sorts.

We're hoping it gets a slot on late-night TV somewhere.

The music certainly loosened Tara up (which was the whole idea of the thing). She told us about her addiction to coke and how she used to bung the equivalent of two large tablespoons up her nose every day. Recently, she said, people had been putting small packets of coke in her handbag, in the hope that she'd fall off the wagon: a photo of her out of her box, she said, would fetch thousands.

She's managed to kick the habit (for the time being anyway) thanks to a spell at a detox clinic in the States. During her first week there she used to go for a run every morning in a pair of tight Lycra shorts and top (which, she said, 'showed my nipples, my *arse*, everything') but she got told off by the management. In future, they said, she could only wear baggy shell suits: the Lycra was making the sex addict contingent, who'd been following her early morning runs closely, overexcited. What a wonderful image that is.

I've been neglecting my portfolio a bit recently: for the first time in ages I only checked the prices once today. And got a bit of a shock.

One of the companies I put £2,500 into – supposedly for the long term – was Transense (makers of early warning systems for tyres that were about to burst). But I sold them for a measly £100 profit after getting all excited over an article about just2clicks in the *FT*.

Well, I made a mistake. In the four weeks since I sold them, Transense shares have gone up. A lot. By more than 300%. From £7.70 to £25. If I'd kept my £2,500 in place it would now be worth nearly £8,000. I feel like I'm watching a plane destined for the Caribbean which I could and should have been on, having at the last minute switched to a weekend in Brighton. Where it's raining.

In fact things are looking a lot less sparky generally. For the second week in a row I'm heading for a loss.

The thing is, as far as Transense is concerned, I broke my own rules: I was going to leave all my investments for the long term. But I had a rush of blood. This is a classic syndrome: everyone has their 'I pulled out on Monday and by the end of the week if I'd stayed in I would've been a millionaire' story. The teachings of the would-be stock market prophet Adam Faith come in handy here. He says, a) it happens to everyone at some stage and b) deciding when to sell is the hardest thing in the world, so c) if you *have* pulled out and made a profit, no matter how small, then you can't say you've done the wrong thing.

'Never turn up your nose at a profit, kid,' he told me.

What's more, things look a little bit worrying on the Autonomy front: the price has sunk from approx. £150 to about £100! That's a drop of a third. I don't know why. There's speculation that the hi-tech party is over; but I don't think it is. Lynchy is due to be quoted on the NASDAQ, the mega American market, in two months, which, if my Football League Theory of stock exchanges holds true, will mean a huge (initial, at least) surge in the share price. If EASDAQ is the stock market's equivalent of the European Champions Cup, NASDAQ is its World Club Champions League. Predicting market movements is notoriously dangerous, but I feel the only way for Autonomy, from here, is up. So I'm bunging half the £30,000 profit I made on Magic Thursday back into it.

I'm also planning to put a sizable wodge of those profits into a company called Kewill Systems, for whom big things are predicted. Here's my sales pitch: last year three billion packages were delivered to people who'd ordered stuff over the Internet. By 2003 it will be twelve billion. Kewill have invented something that helps keep track of every single one of those deliveries. Sounds like a good move to me.

And I really feel I should put some wonga into Oxygen as an act of gratitude, if nothing else: they are doing a lot of work for me, for free (initially, at least).

Oxygen's game plan is quite cute: they go round universities finding out who's got the best e concepts, and then sign up the students there and then. The idea is to take a stake in the companies and help them develop before selling the stake (or part of it) at a huge profit.

One of the blokes behind it is the pasty-faced PR guru Matthew Freud, whose company has managed to get Chris Evans in the papers every day for the last ten years: so getting publicity for the fledgling websites shouldn't be a problem.

Oxygen, you will remember, was the one that shot up to 65p (from 2p) on day one of its flotation: now seems a good time to get in as the price has fallen to less than half that.

Meanwhile I'm beginning to get a grip on things with Sally: I have learned to live with her rejection of me. And I'm starting to realise that I quite like the extra dimension that all this Unrealised Sexual And Emotional Tension is giving our friendship.

Wednesday, 22 March

I have flu.

The publicity bonanza next Monday – the grand launch of the site – is looking good, fingers crossed: the *Independent* look like they'll use my article, and so do the *Guardian*. The *Sun* are sniffing a 'TV man on course to make million' story as well. All three are sending photographers round on Friday to take pictures.

Wonderfully, the *Independent* wants to reproduce the web page as well. Talk about free PR!

I am beginning to feel a bit sorry for Martha and Co. (Her PR lot still won't let me interview her but I'm going to keep trying.)

If Lastminute was a horse, the vets would be eyeing up their rifles.

The share price graph looks like a mountain.

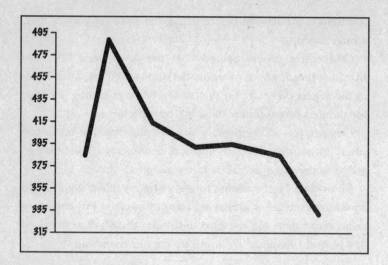

I wouldn't be surprised if it falls even more in the weeks to come. Too much of the wrong kind of publicity can truly be bad for your wealth. This is no bad thing, I think: the punters who got their fingers burned, i.e. bought loads of overpriced shares on the opening day of trading, and then saw their value plummet (like I did with just2clicks), will have learnt a valuable lesson.

Interestingly, I appear to have been right about Autonomy: it went up 20% today.

It seems I may have pulled off the trick of getting to know a share so well that I am correctly identifying the highs – and selling on them – but also recognizing the lows – and buying on those. I promised myself I wouldn't do this but it's just too enticing. I can't resist it.

This is what comes from knowing one company share price intimately. Nice feeling: it's like financial surfing. Same risks, same pleasures.

I am desperate to meet Mike Lynch, by the way: I keep ringing up but no one ever returns my calls. I wonder what he's like.

Am going to Sally's tonight for a cup of tea and a debrief.

Thursday, 23 March

19.30: Am marooned in Manchester doing a report for *Tonight* on banks ripping off their customers, so am having to try to run the whole website project by remote control.

It's still nowhere to be seen: I blame Network Solutions. They are responsible for getting the whole thing up and running. They are a cyberversion of those blokes in white overalls who stand on tall ladders with long brooms and put huge posters up on advertising hoardings. They have my poster but they're not on their ladders yet. At the moment, when I type in the website address www.howtomakeyourmillion.com, I see a cartoon of men with shovels and a sign (in four different languages) saying 'This site is under construction'.

I've also had a momentary worry about people paying for adverts on my site. I worked for the BBC for 15 years so it's ingrained in my consciousness that advertising isn't allowed. But it's not as if I'm endorsing anything. I'm not holding up a packet of soap powder and saying, 'Use this, it's great.' I am publishing something which takes adverts, which is different: like David Dimbleby, who owns a string of local newspapers in South London. So there. (Now I can go round saying that me and David have a lot in common.)

Friday, 24 March

00.45: Just checked to see if website is up and running yet. No, it isn't. Shit. Only 72 hours to go before those articles appear in the papers. And Autonomy is down again. In fact recently it's been up and down like Peter Stringfellow's arse. Should I invest even more at this low point?

07.25: Website still not operational.

09.00: Ditto.

10.00: Ditto.

11.00: Ditto.

12.24: Sally just rang. Do I want to go to Numero Uno's for a meal with her and the kids tonight? Erm, yeah, that would be nice. See you around sevenish?

23.00: Just got back from Sally's after post-meal coffee. I don't think it's ever going to happen between us. I could feel it when I kissed her (on the cheek) goodnight. She's had such a hard time in the past that she doesn't seem willing to put herself in a position where she might get hurt again. I am going to have to be mature and accept that. Which is a pity as a) I am not very mature and b) I find myself wanting to look after her. But I can't tell her about b): it's such a cliché! She is dead attractive too: lovely blue eyes, and a body that is soft and hard in all the right places. And brown as well. And she has no agenda: she is an open book. If she's feeling it, she's showing it; and more often than not saying it too. If I went out with her I could never let her down.

But it's not going to happen.

The new single by the All Saints is fab: it's from the soundtrack to the film *The Beach* and it sounds really, erm . . . beachy. Sally bought it for me today and it's been on heavy rotation ever since. Oh, by the way . . . the shares. I'm down on a couple of weeks ago but it's hardly a disaster. And I'm pretty confident the new additions to the squad – Oxygen, Kewill and more Autonomy – will do the bizzo for me.

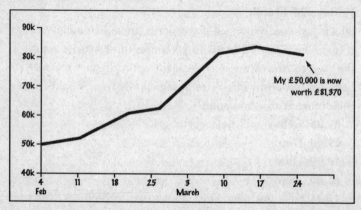

My £50,000 is now worth £81,370

Sunday, 26 March

02.00: Just got back from a Surf 'n' Turf gig: we played my mate Simon's 39th birthday party, at the Hollist Arms in Lodsworth, West Sussex. Am well shagged out . . . driving back was scary, kept feeling like I was about to drop off at the wheel.

Before the gig we played golf (which may explain shaggedness).

I came last. But then I did have two other things on my mind.

Like: 1) How am I going to make this bloody million, share trading? If I'd known about Autonomy a year ago I could have picked up its shares for £4 instead of £60, and I'd have been home and dry by now. If I'd put in £30,000 at that price it would have been worth more than a million by the middle of this month.

If.

I need to find another building with the potential to be a 300-floor skyscraper: but this time I've got to get in at basement level, not the 60th floor.

How the hell am I going to do that?

2) The website. Where the fuck is it?

08.00: Eureka! Sally has left message saying website is up. It's up!

09.00: Well, it is and it isn't. For reasons that I cannot begin to fathom, some people can get it on their PCs, e.g. Sally, her neighbour Debbie and some of her posh chums at the Harbour Club, but here in SW11 I can't, and neither can Dave The Early Bird in North London.

Still, if the above are a representative sample, it sounds like we've got 70% penetration . . . better than 0%.

15.00: Sally is here trying to sort out the website thing. She is now handling all communication between me and Carl TSN, who I think does not like me at all. She asked him all the relevant questions sweetly (How do I measure the number of hits on the site? How do we change the content on it? Why the fuck can't we get it on my screen?) and fielded his explanations patiently. God knows what I would do without her. While she was on the phone I found myself gazing at her, thinking how attractive she was. I hope she didn't notice me. She has a very sexy voice too.

Monday, 27 March

02.00: My birthday. I'm 39. I can't believe it. I'm not young any more. Have just finished working out how to access the website (from Sally's computer, not mine) and 'create content,' i.e. write the stuff that people see on it. Amazing: it's like instant publishing. God knows if anyone will read it, though.

On the site, there are three boxes to fill: I've filled in mine (i.e. my portfolio details), Robin/Hugo has done his (i.e. the weekly share tip) and let's hope Dave in North London (The Early Bird) keeps his end up (i.e. boiled-down version of this morning's financial pages).

The poor git is having to cycle down to the station at King's Cross in the early hours and then spend half the night reading the papers before posting them up on the site in brief.

I hope he'll be OK.

08.00: Got the papers. Oh dear. There is a picture of me plastered all over the back page of the Media *Guardian* wearing a suspect pair of pyjama bottoms. I am also playing the bass. This is a bit embarrassing. My mate Jim has just rung and said it looks appalling. I argued that the pyjama bottoms could pass as a pair of those thick-bloke-from-the-gym-type tracksuit bottoms, as worn by men with huge muscle-bound chests.

I'm all over an entire page of the *Independent*, too.

Two pages in the national press . . . not bad.

If I'd had to pay for adverts taking up the same space, it would have cost me around £120,000. Instead, they're paying me. Not a bad deal.

I think there's a lesson to be learned here: journalists can make quite good dotcom entrepreneurs. The one thing dotcoms need more than anything at the moment is publicity, and publicity is the one thing journalists are good at – it's our job. Dotcoms also need good content – and journalists are good at making that too. They make it every time they write a decent article.

That's probably why there are a stream of top journos flooding out of Fleet Street to help start up Net companies: the industry is long on techno nerds who know how to programme a computer but short of people who can actually fill the websites with anything resembling a decent read.

10.00: At last! Can now get on to my site from my computer. I had to 'clear my cache', whatever that means. The bloke from Gateway told me how to do it, over the phone. I felt a bit like a passenger who'd taken the wheel of a jumbo in midair being talked down by air traffic control. They charged me a pound a minute for the privilege: disgraceful. Anyway, the site looks rather attractive: the only problem is that Dave (The Early Bird) from North London has taken the unilateral decision to print the contents of the financial pages from Sunday's (i.e. yesterday's) papers, and not this morning's, as they're a bit thin and don't contain any share tips.

Not a good idea. The Internet is supposed to be up to the minute, and we're more like 24 hours behind. But I can't be arsed to do anything about it now . . . at least we're up and running.

11.00: More publicity on the way: the *Daily Mirror* want to interview me and Radio 2 and Radio Ireland want to chat as well. Why not? All publicity is good publicity.

I think.

18.00: Did Johnny Walker on Radio 2. The bloke who had an unfortunate incident involving him, the *News of the World* and some cocaine allegations. He ended by saying, 'I bet all your mates think you're really boring now.' I said, 'Yes, but not half as boring as you, Johnny.' I had very much wanted to say, 'Why don't you invest in Coke, Johnny?' And then leave a gap of approx. one and a half seconds, before adding, '. . . as in Coca-Cola: they're doing very well', but I didn't have the balls.

18.45: Just done half an hour with Eamonn Dunphy on Radio Ireland. It was great: I really enjoyed it.

His claim to fame is that when he was a pro footballer (he used to play for Charlton, funnily enough) he once posed for a team photograph, seated, thighs splayed, unaware that a bollock was hanging out of the right side of his shorts. I reminded him of this during the interview and he laughed it off (in a professional kind of way).

The irony is that I'm now being presented as some kind of Internet guru, when I know fuck all about it. Mind you, ignorance of a subject has never held me back before. Eamonn asked me if, in my opinion, the Internet would mean the death of newspapers, so I answered him. (No, I didn't think so: you can't read the Internet on the train, can you?).

23.45: Just got back from Sally's. She threw a dinner party for me. Richard (Normal) came, and we took the piss out of him for a good ten minutes about his family firm's website (they refurbish pubs). It consists of six slightly fuzzy pictures of tables and chairs and not much else.

Sally looked gorgeous and laid on vast amounts of lamb and beef and stuff. Vast quantities of champagne were quaffed.

On a scale of 1–10, where 1 is sober and 10 is smashed, I'm a 6.

Nowadays, whenever I kiss Sally goodnight (cheek, not lips), I can't help imbuing it with a bit of firmness: it's more than a peck. I'm sure she notices.

I wonder what she thinks.

Tuesday, 28 March

14.00: Got call from Sally while filming. Ohmigod. The data for the website has come through, for the first day. It got 32,000 hits

– 32,000! Fuck. That is a lot. That doesn't mean 32,000 different people logged on, though: hits aren't people. Because there are three different images on the site, each time a person logs on that counts as 3 hits. Still: we're off to a flyer.

And that's got to be good news when it comes to persuading more advertisers to come on board.

Sally says I have bucketfuls of e-mails too, thanks to the magic of the Net: all you have to do is click on my name, which is on the bottom of the site, and I get the message.

I have been reading a book (*Striking it Rich.Com: profiles of 23 incredibly successful websites you've probably never heard of*) which says how crucial it is to 'nurture your customers', i.e. reply to each and every one of their e-mails, individually and lovingly. So that's what I'm going to do.

23.30: The Internet has changed my life: I've just been reading e-mails from old friends I haven't seen for years, and from people I don't know, saying the warmest, nicest things ('Heard you on the radio today . . . Good on you, mate, for having the balls . . . hope you make your million . . . yours, Ray O'Malley'). There are also ones that could lead to even bigger things: a bloke called Michael Lusada, the CEO of a company called equitytracker.com, wants a meeting. He sounds like a rich, flash-suited Wall Street type. Should be interesting.

One bloke has sent me his CV and asked for a job.

There's also a slightly worrying one from a bloke called Desmond Chin, from the Financial Services Authority. They are the government body who regulate people who run financial websites.

In his e-mail, Mr Chin says: 'I need to talk.'

He wants a Chin wag.

This is ironic: if you log on to Moneyworld, the name of one of the biggest financial websites there is, using the suffix '.com' instead of '.co.uk', you don't get stocks and shares, you get lurid colour close-ups of women and men (and the occasional animal) having sex. It's a porn site. With headlines like 'Live Fucking from Amsterdam!!! Only 6 dollars!'. You'd have thought Mr Chin would be paying more attention to them than to me.

But then again maybe he is.

Wednesday, 29 March
11.00: Just got back from the Akash. Feeling very pleased with myself as I managed to talk about something other than You Know What for over an hour.

The Dreaded Mr Chin from the Financial Services Authority called today . . . he wants to meet me on Tuesday. The government are on to me!

I need to take a lawyer so I'm going with Sally's mate, Anne from Vauxhall. The problem appears to be that my site is offering investment advice and to do that I need a licence. And getting a licence isn't easy. You need to be a qualified independent financial adviser, for a start.

I'm assuming they can't pull the plug on me, though — i.e. take me off the Net — as they don't have the power. That's because government legislation hasn't kept up with developments on the Internet. Which is why there are so many sites about offering pictures of men/women/animals/vegetables/household implements. Even so, I hope we can find a way through this as the FSA could make life *very* difficult indeed for me if they wanted to. They can't take my ball away from me now, surely?

Every day brings fresh reminders of how the Internet has changed my life. On days I'm not working I spend hours in front of this screen, answering e-mails from people I haven't met, looking at share prices, and updating my site. I now smoke 20 a day, eat even more crap food than I used to, and often sleep just four hours a night. I've become boring and obsessed; I think about the project every single second of my waking days. I dream about it too.

I am going to try to enjoy the whole thing more: but it's

difficult to smell the roses when you've developed a smoker's cough, a spare tyre, bags under your eyes, and feel like you're mentally chained to a radiator.

And I really must find some more killer investments. I am posting the results of month two up on the website tomorrow and it's not looking very good at all. I am supposed to be in this for the long term, I know: if some of my investments do a *Titanic* I must be prepared to go down with them, saluting all the way. But I'm beginning to think that in one or two cases I should be thinking about jumping ship.

Having said that I would gladly forfeit making the million if it meant I could go out with Sally. I've started fancying her so much it's doing my head in. It's not like seeing someone tasty in a crowded room whom you find attractive: I fancy her from the inside out. The other night she kissed me on the cheek as I left her house and for the first time ever I became aware of feeling (ahem) the top part of her body pushing gently against mine. She is part cheerleader, part Kathleen Turner. Woof!

Saturday, 1 April

11.00: Oh dear. I have just done my sums. I have lost £10,000 in the last month. High-tech Internet shares have taken a complete pasting: investors have woken up to the fact that some of them are absurdly overvalued. Curiously I don't feel too panicky: although I did feel slightly worried when I saw a bailiff's van drive past my house this morning. For one fleeting moment I thought they might be coming for me. The thing is, I reckon this crash/correction is A Good Thing: it will sort out the wheat from the chaff. People will now become more picky about what they invest in: instead of throwing dosh at anything with a dotcom in the title, they will actually exercise a bit of judgment. Some Internet companies – the ones that are a bit shit – will never recover from this: they have been found out. The good ones, on the other hand, will survive and, ultimately, get stronger. Very Darwinian. Here's how things look:

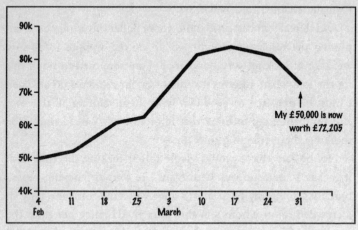

My £50,000 is now worth £72,205

NAME OF CO.	INITIAL STAKE	SHARE PRICE THEN	SHARE PRICE NOW	WHAT'S MY STAKE WORTH NOW, THEN?
Autonomy 1	£30,000	£58.55	£99.75	£29,300*
Autonomy 2	£15,000	£102	£99.75	£14,650
Kewill	£10,000	£19.75	£14.68	£7,420
Oxygen	£2,500	25p	13p	£1,270
Charlton	£2,500	54p	63p	£2,875
MV Sports	£2,500	4p	2p	£1,250
Birchin	£2,500	12p	6p	£1,250
just2clicks	£2,500	£2.68	£1.25	£1,190
Airtel	£2,500	38p	30p	£1,980
Monotub	£2,500	£2.70	£4.40	£4,250
Monticello	£2,500	£1.10	83p	£1,840
4Front	£2,500	£14.90	£14.50	£2,430
Cash Reserves	£2,500			£2,500
TOTAL				£72,205

*Figure takes into account £30,000 of 'profit taking' on Magic Thursday

Looking at my shares individually I have to say that going for Monticello, on the basis of a tip from a fat bloke at the dogs, was not the best of ideas. I bought at £1.10: the price has now slumped to 83p and I am getting out. I am also selling Monotub, but for different reasons. They've done great, and gone up from £2.70 to £4.40, an increase of more than 50% – and even though I was planning to hold on to them all year I can hardly turn my nose up at such a fat profit. (Thanks, Adam.)

With the proceeds from these two I am now going to shell out on two more tasty-looking prospects:

1) Nike. They recently announced poor profit figures: the share price slumped massively. So much so – says my mate Timo, the inventor of Beard Theory – that they are now far cheaper than they should be.

2) Pace. This lot are at the cutting edge of development at the place where computers meet television. One day, the two boxes will merge: there will be just the one big 'un, in the corner of your room, that gives you the lot: TV progs, e-mails, share price info, everything. When that happens Pace will coin it. And in the meantime, I hope, so will I.

Meanwhile there are some other poorly-looking patients in the sick bay. MV Sports and Birchin are now both down by more than 30%.

But I'm hoping they'll come back. If I'm honest I was rather attracted to them because they were cheap (4p and 12p respectively), but now it seems that may have been a very good reason to have avoided them entirely: a lot of experts say that so-called 'penny shares' are a nightmare waiting to happen and anything under 50p should be treated with extreme caution.

But I'm not really panicking as much as I might: this cloud has a bit of a silver lining. The way I see it, the more precarious my finances, the more people will log on to my website, to see how I'm doing.

That should make it more valuable. We have now had 130,000 hits in the last week, helped by a phenomenal amount of free publicity: this morning, for instance, I am splashed across two pages of the *Daily Mirror*. (The article contains wonderful factual inaccuracies like 'half the population of Britain are now buying and selling stocks and shares over the Internet'. Oops. 'Half the population' is 30 million people: at present, only 5 million are hooked up to the Net.

I've worked out that in the past week I've had approximately half a million pounds' worth of free advertising. If I'd had to pay for an advert the size of today's article in the *Mirror*, for instance, it would have cost me £80,000.

A bit of rat-like cunning helps too: I got the piece in the *Mirror* by ringing up their show business editor, Richard Wallace, whom I used to know when I worked at BBC Radio Oxford, and telling him that the *Sun* were interested. Actually, the *Sun* weren't that interested, but there's nothing a tabloid hack likes more than getting one over his rivals.

16.00: My God. I've just had a very interesting phone call, from a bloke called John Sewell. He runs a company called Phase8. They buy up websites, develop them, and sell them on at a profit. The conversation went something like this:

JS: 'We are preparing a list of sites we want to auction, you know . . . and we have lots of PLCs with lots of money who might want to snap them up. Why don't you put yours on our list?'

JM (trying to sound calm): 'Hmm, OK, I don't see why not. How much do you think it's worth?'

JS: 'I'd put it up for sale for five million.'

Five million? Five million? My website is going to be put up for sale for £5 million? Who on earth is going to shell out that kind of dosh?

Mind you, I'm not going to argue with him. And I suppose there is a possibility that a big company with deep pockets might come in with an offer. I read recently, for instance, that gambling via the Internet is going to be the next big thing: the market is going to be worth £5 billion over the next five years, apparently. If you were going for a piece of that market, and you had several million quid in your budget, and you wanted to get yourself established, why not spend a chunk of it buying up a website with a) a gambler-friendly name (like mine), b) a sizeable, loyal clientèle (like mine) and c) huge appeal to people who like a flutter (like mine)?

What's more, the site is making a real cash profit, too: one of the few websites in the world to be doing so, as far as I can tell. This is thanks to the £5,000 deal with PPP. It lasts for three months: the total running costs of the site for that period will be less than £3,000 (i.e. the dosh and expenses I'm paying to Dave The Early Bird and Hugo). So that's two grand of pure profit.

Yesterday's meeting with Michael Lusada was rather thought-provoking too: I was expecting a flash Yank but he turned out to be a posh Brit who looked like a slightly pasty-faced version of Rob Lowe. He too is taking a bit of a gamble. He has left his steady job in banking to start his own company: the idea is to start a financial website called equitytracker.com. I'm not sure his timing is great, though: right now, what the world really doesn't need is a) yet another dotcom company and b) yet another financial website.

But he's got a few hundred grand behind him, and he believes in his idea enough to have personally run up a six-figure overdraft. Another advertiser perhaps?

Sunday, 2 April
Sally is going to the States for three weeks with her kids and wants to keep in constant contact, so I'm buying her a laptop computer.

We went to PC World to get one this morning and who should be there, trying to sell us one, but Imran, Mr Samad's son (as in The Worst Corner Shop In The Universe, ever). Imran seemed to have brought a little bit of his dad's reverse magic with him; the laptop we wanted wasn't in stock, and neither was the second one we chose. We ended up wasting an hour there: we've now decided to buy one over the Internet instead.

Tuesday, 4 April

Today I met the government. The Financial Services Authority, to be precise. I was with Anne from Vauxhall, Sally's mate, who has now been drafted in as the company lawyer, in return for 1% of the company. We discussed tactics in the reception of FSA HQ, a huge, antiseptic skyscraper in Canary Wharf, while we waited to be taken up to Floor 14.

The job of the FSA is to protect the small investor. For the small investor's sake I hope they're better at finance than they are at English: a huge cloth poster in reception, which consisted of a very long poem, contained no less than six basic spelling errors.

We were met by a thirtysomething bloke called Matthew Aarons. He reminded me of the sort of bloke I used to take the piss out of at school: small, self-contained, and ever so slightly pompous. The sort of pomposity that people who know they're quite intelligent have. He was pleasant, though. I made a point of being chatty and friendly to him.

We bonded, slightly, I felt, following a joint slagging off of Lastminute.com. If nothing else that company has performed a magnificent service to the nation, uniting on the one hand the millions who are now going round saying 'I Told You So', and on the other the (ever decreasing) number of others who are saying 'You Just Wait'.

The three of us were joined round the table in a small glass office by an Australian-sounding lawyer who didn't say much and looked pretty bored.

Mr Aarons got straight to the point. He wasn't being friendly any more. The primary purpose of my website, he said, was to give financial advice. As such, it needed to be licensed by the FSA. It wasn't. Therefore it was in breach of the Financial Services Act.

'Do you know the penalties for that?' he asked.

'No.'

'Two years in prison and a hefty fine.'

That's a bit stiff, I thought. People are putting pictures of men buggering animals on the Web and getting away with it and I'm being threatened with the clinker for allegedly offering people financial advice.

My mother had a novel approach to the problems of being confronted by the authorities: once, when Epsom and Ewell Borough Council told her that guests at her hotel shouldn't be using the carpark in the park opposite, she wrote back and told them that her guests were doing 'a lot less harm than the people who take their dogs there to fill the place full of shit so why don't you go and fuck yourselves. Your sincerely, Mrs Maitland'.

Not a tactic to be using here, I decided.

'OK, what can we do to make you lot happy?'

After twenty minutes we came to a reasonably satisfactory compromise: I would modify the content of the site to make it less stock market-oriented and more about the Internet generally. That seemed to placate them a bit. But it was by no means a green light. They would continue to monitor the site, they said, and reserved the right to close it down, if they didn't like what they saw. I didn't want to drop my trousers and bend over the table completely, i.e. take all the advice off the site completely, as it might make it less attractive . . . but on the other hand bending a little in their direction seemed the sensible thing to do. And looking on the bright side, broadening the content might actually make the site more appealing to a greater number of people.

So in a way, the FSA have done us a bit of a favour really. I changed the content of the site over my mobile, in the taxi, on the way home. A bit like a newspaper editor who's at dinner rearranging his front page when a big story breaks late at night. Quite exciting really.

I'm a little worried about what's happening out there in the market. Michael Buerk was on the *Nine o'Clock News* tonight saying, in that slightly annoying doom-laden way of his: 'There are fears of a stock market crash tonight, following the US courts' judgment against Microsoft [sharp and very audible intake of breath, almost a hissing sound]. Bill Gates, meanwhile, vows to fight on.'

The report that followed related how Bill Gates had lost his latest court battle (Microsoft had been accused of anti-competitive behaviour) and, for some reason I don't fully understand, alleged that everyone in the States was now selling their hi-tech stocks. Prices were tumbling there, and there were signs that the same thing was starting to happen here. The herd is on the move! I am not going to panic, though: I am going to be strong.

I also read a very interesting article in *Private Eye*. It was about the effect that certain high-profile City 'stars' like Nigel Wray and Luke Johnson (of Pizza Express) have on share prices. Particularly Internet share prices. The gist of it was this: the stars buy shares in boring, old-fashioned companies which then announce they're going to reinvent themselves as exciting new dotcom outfits. The share price explodes upwards as the herd move in, chanting 'Luke is in! Nigel is in!'

But, the article said, often, by the time the herd is in, Nigel, Luke and chums are out – and sitting on fat profits.

It gave, as an example, a company called Blake's Clothing. A few months ago its shares shot up from a few pennies to well over £2 on the news that it was to become a dotcom. Not long afterwards Luke Johnson sold loads of his shares in the company for more than £800,000. He hadn't done anything wrong, mind you: making money out of other investors on the basis of your reputation isn't a crime. What he said at the time, though, was interesting: 'Shares are for selling. There's a lot of speculation and fingers will be burned.' Hmmm.

I hope his words aren't about to come true . . .

Wednesday, 5 April
18.00: Oh dear. For the first time ever, I am a bit scared. Hi-tech and Internet stocks appear to be falling off the cliff. I have lost £8,000 in the first three days of this week alone. I lost ten grand last week: at this rate, I will be waving goodbye to my entire 50k by the end of next month.

What worries me is that no one seems to know when, or if, this fall is going to slow down, or stop. Everyone who has been living it up at the Hotel Internet recently seems to be heading for the door marked 'exit'.

As far as I can tell, this seems to have been caused by: 1) the Bill Gates incident and 2) people taking a closer look at some of the absurd valuations of hi-tech and Internet companies and realising that what all the wise old hands have been saying all along might have more than a grain of truth in it.

The trouble is, everyone (like me) bought hi-tech stocks earlier this year because – er – everyone else was. Now everyone's selling, for the same reason.

Ironically, and with superb timing, the computer software that the entire City relies on to keep it running also crashed today: the market couldn't open till late afternoon, and so no one could actually trade a single share for seven hours. How very appropriate. In the week when investors have started to lose faith in high-technology shares big time, the high technology that enables them to invest in the first place goes and proves their judgment right by spectacularly and very publicly breaking down.

My hope is that this is all A Good Thing; people will now search out the proper companies, with real growth prospects, and turn away from the dross, which will wither and die (it's what the City lot call 'a flight to quality', apparently).

But the signs are not good: it looks a bit like a baby and bath water scenario. Autonomy, surely a quality company if ever there was one (surely?), is down to £65. It has fallen by more than 50% in the last ten days.

What is going on? I still feel I should be strong, and not panic: to bail out and sell now would be to admit defeat, to go with the herd. This is the hardest decision any first-time investor has to make. The question 'When is the right time to sell?' is the most difficult one of all, and no one can ever give a definitive answer to it.

It's particularly hard making up your mind when your shares are plummeting. If they're going up, and you sell, even if they carry on rising afterwards, it's hardly a disaster: no one ever went bust by taking profits too early. But a lot of experts reckon that once a share starts falling, you should get out. Many argue you should have a 'stop loss' policy in place: i.e. when the thing falls a certain amount – by more than 10%, let's say – you automatically bail out.

Share prices fall for a reason, they argue. It may well be that key players in the market have come to the conclusion that your company is not going to be the shining star they once thought. And who are you to argue?

I was reading Andrew Alexander, the Wise Old Investment Owl who writes for the *Daily Mail*, the other day. He argues that selling at a loss might hurt your pride, but investing is about boosting your capital, not your ego.

There are three plus points to be had from selling, he reckons:

1) you're free from the stress of having to check the thing every 30 seconds, 2) you also have a pile of cash which will not go down in value while you look for a better share to put it on, and 3) you have a loss to set against future capital gains tax bills.

All very persuasive. Andrew Alexander certainly seems to know what he's talking about. He may not have a beard but he has a credibility-boosting bow tie and looks like he's been around for donkey's years. But I reckon this is just a case of the 'new economy' being temporarily out of favour. I still think Something Significant is happening out there: there just seems to have been a big pause for breath. For a kick-off, lots of dotcom companies that were due to float in the next few weeks are now postponing, or calling off, their flotations altogether; the better ones, however, will eventually come to market. But that's good: no more free money. Mind you, in Holland there has been a very revealing incident indeed: one of the directors of a big Internet company there is being threatened with legal action by angry investors.

This is because she has quietly sold her shares, for much less than their face value, thus earning herself a small fortune. (It only came to light after people went through her company's prospectus with a fine-tooth comb and realised, after reading the small print, what she'd done.) This is not good for the morale and confidence of the people investing in that company: if someone who is supposed to be leading it, and believing in it, sells her shares for far less than they're supposedly worth, it tends to make the whole thing look like an exercise in money-making and not much else. There seems to be one almighty reality check going on out there.

Thursday, 6 April
07.00: Have just had the definitive anxiety dream: a nightmare that Mike Lynch shaved his beard off.

Friday, 7 April

Phew! The worst seems to be over. Autonomy has made a significant recovery. The storm has passed. But it's done some damage:

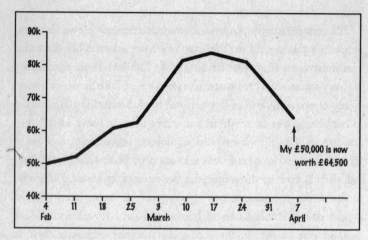

My £50,000 is now worth £64,500

Stockmarket missile heading for my house which, if current conditions continue, will reduce entire structure to rubble, very soon

MISSILE

Remains of patio I was planning in my head following successes of first month

Sunday, 9 April

More evidence that I've started a trend: the *Sunday Times* business section has started a weekly feature written by a bloke who is mortgaging his house to buy and sell stocks and shares on the Internet. He has a beard.

The words 'imitation' and 'flattery' come to mind. Soon hordes of glinty-eyed crazed homeowners will be descending on their local mortgage providers, looking to put their houses and families on the line. I don't think this is such a bad thing, actually. With the abundance of information now available to us all through the Internet, we, the great unwashed, are arguably in as good a position as the professionals to make key investment decisions. In fact, given that it's our own money we're talking about, we might even end up making better decisions than them. Let's face it, you're going to be far more careful about investing your own money than someone else will.

Want the evidence? Well, at the moment there are no less than three million people with endowment mortgages who are facing the prospect that the lump sum they're going to get at the end of it may not be enough to pay back the sum they originally borrowed. This is appalling and a national scandal. It's happened because the 'professionals' who have invested the mortgage payments – in the stock market – have cocked it up.

OK, so we might end up cocking it up too, but at least we will have had the satisfaction of losing our own money ourselves, rather than letting some failed public schoolboy in a suit lose it for us.

There has always been a tendency, I think, to assume that just because a bloke sounds posh and works in the City, he knows what he's doing.

The other day I was talking, on the phone, to a stockbroker who wanted my business. (I was thinking of buying into a company whose shares I couldn't get via the Internet.) He sounded like he was in his early 40s, and his accent was pure Terry-Thomas. We talked about that company: his firm, supposedly, specialised in it. I had done my homework on them and quoted a few facts and figures. He sounded surprised. ('. . . Gosh! . . . Golly! . . .') It was clear he knew less than I did about the company. Worrying, given that his job was to advise people on how to invest huge chunks of their money.

They say the Internet is bringing power back to the people. I doubted that at one time, but now I think I know what they mean.

Thursday, 13 April

Time for another strategy: A Very High Risk One Indeed. If I'm serious about the million – and I am – I have to do this: for High Rewards you have to take High Risks.

Spread betting is High Risk. It's in the news at the moment. Hanse Cronje, the South African cricket captain, has just resigned after admitting taking money from a spread betting bookie.

The first thing you have to realise about spread betting on the stock market is that it's got nothing to do with good, old-fashioned, sensible investment. It's gambling, pure and simple. Very scary gambling, too: anyone who gets involved should buy a pair of tungsten-reinforced brown trousers first.

But it's catching on, big time: and getting its claws into people. Gambling helplines say newly obsessed spread betting addicts are coming forward every day. Those addicts are attracted by two things: 1) the fact that you can win (in theory) unlimited amounts of money, and 2) that it's all tax free.

There is a downside, of course: the potential losses can be unlimited too. The basic principle of spread betting is that the more right you are, the more you win. The more wrong you are, the more you lose.

This is how it works. You pick a company: Akash plc. You have heard that they are 'one of the best Indian restaurants in Clapham Junction' and you think they have a rosy future. The share price is 100p. You think it will go to 150p by next Friday. Now you find out what 'the spread' is. You ring the bookie who says it's 90p–110p. This is very important: it means the bookie thinks that by next Friday Akash will go no lower than 90p, and no higher than 110p. You disagree: and you bet £100 a penny on it.

This means that if the share exceeds the bookie's expectations – and goes up beyond 110p – you start making money: beyond this point, every penny it goes up, you make £100.

So: if it goes to 120p, it's exceeded the upper spread limit of 110p by 10p. So you make 10 × £100 = £1000. If it goes all the way to 150p, bingo: £4,000. This is called 'buying' the Akash.

The bad news, of course, is that if the price falls, you lose. Let's say it goes to 65p: that's 45p short of the limit that you bet it would beat. So: you lose 45 × £100: £4,500.

A few other things to be aware of: 1) you can bet on shares going down as well as up (this is called 'selling'); 2) you can lay a 'controlled risk bet' i.e. if your losses reach a certain point, the bet automatically shuts down and the bookie walks off with your dosh.

Needless to say the spread betting firms like to make out that loads of people have made spectacular fortunes in no time at all. They may well have.

But many more will have lost them.

One of the most spectacular success stories involved a City trader who had been betting for a few weeks on the Dow Jones index going down. It had been: he'd made himself sixty grand. Nice. One day he decided to risk the lot. He bet £600 a point on it going down even farther. But he also introduced a controlled risk element: if it went up just 100 points, the bet would cancel itself and he would lose his entire sixty grand.

That day, it went down 500 points. He made £350,000.

Six months later he retired.

You can spread bet on anything: the number of times a cricket umpire is going to give someone out LBW, the number of corners in a football match, even the number of times Barry Davies says 'I have to say . . .' in one of his football commentaries.

When it comes to sport, though, the opportunities for corruption are endless . . . and that's where Hanse Cronje, the South African cricket captain, comes in.

There was an interesting episode recently during a football game: a huge amount of money was put on there being a throw-in within the first 20 seconds. The match kicked off, and one of the players immediately booted the ball into touch. Hmm.

During the recent rugby World Cup one leading international team apparently clubbed together to put a massive bet on one of their players – a very well-known one – carrying the ball more times than anyone else in the team. Surprise, surprise, he got the thing passed to him at every available moment. He ended up being the most prolific ball-carrier by a mile and the team ended up making a packet.

I've thought about doing a spread bet for a long time; I just haven't had the balls. But I have now. Autonomy is lower than it's been for weeks: about £70. I'm sure it's going to go up. I am putting £800 a point on it. So every pound it goes up, I'll make £800. I reckon – I hope – it should go to around £80, judging by its past performance, quite soon. In which case (allowing for the spread) I'll pocket close to seven grand. The bet gets called in next Tuesday night, unless I elect to close it off before then.

14.30: Not doing too bad. It's already up to £75. If I called it off now I'd be £2,500 better off . . .

15.15: Even better. It's £78. Very close to my target . . . I could call it in now and make close to six grand! But I'm hanging on in there.

16.01: The market has closed and Autonomy has tumbled. *Shit!* Down to £74. I can't cash in my chips now (I'd make a profit of 2k) even if I wanted to: they will only let you do that when the market is open.

Friday, 14 April
15.00: Have checked the markets every half-hour and it's been slowly sliding. Now down to £70. Shitshitshit. I *wish* I'd sold yesterday and taken the 6k. If I sold now, I'd lose £4,000.

I'm just going to have to hope things rebound before next Tuesday night or I'll have another mini-disaster on my hands.

23.45: Sally has sent me an e-mail from the States. She said she's just read an article headlined 'Waiting for a stock to rebound isn't investment, it's DENIAL'. That's my problem: I just can't bring myself to sell my plummeting shares, because I'm convinced they'll rebound.

It's that stop loss thing again . . . it makes sense, I know, but I feel like I've invested emotionally in my shares, not just financially: to sell now would be like calling off a three-month relationship just because you've had an argument with your girlfriend about her appalling, interfering parents (i.e. logic tells you 'This could well be a problem' but pride says 'If I call it off now I'll feel like a failure and why waste the last three months?'). Hope springs eternal, I guess. Sentimentality is the enemy of the good investor, I know, but I just can't help it.

The carnage among the hi-tech stocks is continuing: what seems to be happening is that, as usual, the US markets are leading, and we are following.

As the saying goes: when America sneezes, we catch a cold.

(Or in my case pneumonia.)

Apart from people suddenly deciding that hi-tech stocks are ludicrously overvalued over there, something else significant is going on: the 'lock-in period' for directors of loads of dotcom companies is now expiring. The 'lock-in period' is the time during which major stakeholders in companies are unable to sell their (usually) massive stakes. Normally directors are locked in for 12 straight months, starting on day one of the public flotation.

A lot of the big dotcom companies in the US were floated around 12 months ago. And now, guess what: loads of directors who've spent the past year saying 'This company has a riilllly great future' are now selling vast chunks of their shares in it, as quickly as possible.

Lots of other investors are, of course, then selling too; if they see the people who started the company in the first place making off with the loot, why should they hang around and be left with a worthless bundle of rags?

It's all very worrying.

Saturday, 15 April

09.14: Oh my God. I have just opened a letter from the spread betting company I'm with. It is a bill. It has lots of figures on it. At the bottom there is a figure, preceded by the words 'The amount now due for immediate payment is . . .'

It is a big figure. Hey. It's OK. It's a misprint. It must be. It has to be. The sum is 21,709.85p.

Twenty-one thousand, seven hundred and nine pounds, eighty-five pence. I owe them more than twenty thousand pounds. Twenty thousand pounds.

And they want their twenty thousand pounds right now.

Except I haven't got twenty thousand pounds right now.

There must be a mistake. They have got the decimal point in the wrong place. I am breathing even harder now: for the first time this year I am genuinely scared. This is horrible. I can feel the fear in my throat and in my stomach.

12.15: Have phoned the company: it's not quite as bad as I thought but it's still pretty terrible and it could get much worse.

My Autonomy spread bet has gone badly out of control: I am £7,220 down on it. The figure of twenty thousand is what they want me to send (now) to cover any further losses. I'm not going to: I haven't got the money!

13.00: I never used to read stories in the papers about share price crashes: I would occasionally skim them, with amused detachment, thinking how it served the bastards right.

That was then, this is now. Today, in the *Daily Mail*, in big black letters, which take up most of the page, the headline screams 'SHARES IN RECORD PLUNGE ON WALL STREET'. Farewell, amused detachment, hello, wide-eyed horror.

14.15: I have a plan: it's a dangerous one, but it might work. (It fucking has to!) I think I may do a hedge bet. Here goes: on Monday, I will place a spread bet on the EASDAQ market falling overall. (That's the market Autonomy is on.) There is a figure, given in points, that shows how all the companies on the EASDAQ are doing as a whole. On Friday, at 5 p.m., it closed at 1,640 points (roughly 100 down for the day). But in the three hours that followed, the New York markets sank alarmingly . . . and carried on sinking. Everything points to the EASDAQ following suit on Monday, especially as it is a market specifically for hi-tech companies: and hi-techs are taking the biggest battering of all at the moment (and have been, for three weeks). So I think I am going to take a spread bet on it doing just that. At the moment it is 1,640 points. If I bet £300 on every point it goes down, and it falls another 100 points, I make £30,000. But it might not be as easy as that: the buy–sell spread might be unkind to me. My thinking is this: if the EASDAQ plummets, Autonomy will too, and I will lose even more thousands.

But if I have a simultaneous bet, which makes me money if the EASDAQ goes down, I will be, as they say in the City, 'hedged'. That's the theory, anyway. But there is a nightmare scenario: I could lose big on both bets, in which case my entire fifty grand will be wiped out, and I'll be left owing another few grand to boot. I have a feeling that this could be The Defining Moment Of This Ludicrous Experiment.

Monday, 17 April

VERY BLACK MONDAY BUT IN RETROSPECT IT COULD HAVE BEEN EVEN WORSE AND AT LEAST I'VE LEARNED SOMETHING (OR MAYBE I HAVEN'T).

07.59: Am on phone to spread betting company, having not slept all night. Normally, when I'm having trouble nodding off, watching the BBC's News 24 channel does the trick for me instantly: last night I found myself watching the 3.30 a.m. report from the Tokyo stock market more avidly than the dénouement to a Hitchcock thriller.

08.03: Have got through: I owe them £8,000. It could have been worse, I suppose. I am going to hang on in there and hope it rebounds.

08.04: Check share price again. There is a red arrow next to it. Pointing downwards. For several seconds I sit, motionless and scared, with my head in my hands. What am I going to do? This is a nightmare. How the hell did it come to this? It's eight o'clock in the morning and I am losing thousands by the minute.

Suddenly I am aware of a wet, sweet taste on the index finger of my right hand. It is blood. I have chewed a third of the nail, and the surrounding skin, clean away.

08.05: Enough is enough. I have closed the bet. When you're this far in over your head it's the only sensible option. Curiously, my overriding emotion now is one of relief. I've only lost £8,000. Only irony is, I feel like I've got off lightly: at £8,000!

But you have to remember that at one stage (around 4.23 a.m. actually,) in theory, I could easily have lost not only my initial 50k investment, but another 50k on top of that.

So: what have I learned? Well, Spread Betting Is To Be Avoided

At All Costs. The whole thing is (surprise, surprise) heavily loaded against the punter: because of the spread system, you could actually bet on a share going up, see it then go up, close the bet, and still lose money. So, a word of advice for those thinking of having a go: don't.

PS: I am now going to burn my spread betting membership card on a funeral pyre in the kitchen.

09.00: PPS: Just as well I got out when I did. Autonomy has now dropped 25% in just 60 minutes. If I'd stayed in, I'd now be twenty grand down on that one bet.

While all this has been going on, in Washington there have been ugly clashes in the streets between anarchists and the police, at a meeting of the International Monetary Fund. Blood has been spilt! (though not as much as in my portfolio). The IMF have tried to calm everyone down: what sparked off this crash was a worrying set of American inflation forecasts, but, the IMF assures us, there is nothing to get too panicky about.

If they took a look at the state of my house, mind you, they might be singing a different tune:

Chimney fallen down, and half of roof now
blown away due to severe turbulence
(emanating from America)

I'm not including my spread betting losses in my investment portfolio table, though, because (as I said before) spread betting ain't investment: it's gambling. I will account for the losses eventually: but in a separate table, which will include *all* my Internet/ Stock Market Spin-Off activities: the profits (from advertising, and writing) and the losses (from spread betting, and maintaining the site).

Mind you: my investment portfolio looks truly shocking anyway, regardless of the spread betting fiasco. It's now the lowest it's been all year: it's worth £43,000. It's almost halved, in just over a month. I've lost £40,000 in five weeks. There's one consolation: a loss is only a loss when you decide to sell. And I'm not selling. And anyway: it's only money.

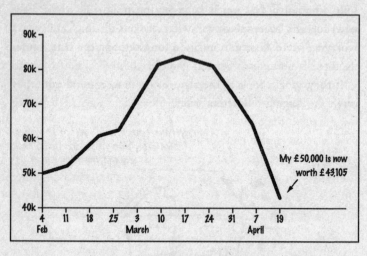

My £50,000 is now worth £43,105

NAME OF CO.	INITIAL STAKE	SHARE PRICE THEN	SHARE PRICE NOW	WHAT'S MY STAKE WORTH NOW, THEN?
Autonomy 1	£30,000	£58.55	£46.10	£13,520*
Autonomy 2	£15,000	£102	£46.10	£6,760
Kewill	£10,000	£19.75	£12.21	£6,015
Oxygen	£2,500	25p	10p	£1,000

Charlton	£2,500	54p	60p	£2,760
MV Sports	£2,500	4p	1.5p	£950
Birchin	£2,500	12p	4p	£830
just2clicks	£2,500	£2.68	£1.19	£1,140
Airtel	£2,500	38p	29p	£1,930
4Front	£2,500	£19.90	£11.10	£1,740
Pace	£2,500	£11.09	£6.90	£1,580
Nike	£2,500	£18.00	£25.20	£3,380
Cash Reserves	£1,500			£1,500
TOTAL				£43,105

* Takes into account £30,000 profits I took on Magic Thursday

Tuesday, 18 April

I may not have the best investment record in the world right now but I'm certainly a good story: today I've done interviews with two national radio stations in Ireland, and been rung up by the Dutch version of the *Financial Times*, who are doing a feature on me. One of the Irish interviewers was Eamonn Dunphy, of bollocks-hanging-out-of-his-shorts fame: he wants to have me on every fortnight now. For some reason people in Ireland in particular are really getting into this thing. I'm also writing a mega-feature for the *Mail on Sunday* this weekend: I appear to have caught the public's imagination. I guess people are getting vicarious pleasure out of seeing someone else act so dangerously: they can experience the highs and lows, but without having to go through the traumas I'm going through. Come to think of it, yesterday I even made front-page news: I'd written a short piece for the *Daily Express*, and when I went to Mr Samad's to buy a copy, I found him reading one. 'Look,' he said, pointing at the front page. There, across the top, underneath the *Express* title, in whacking great letters, next to a mugshot of yours truly, was the headline 'I've gambled everything to make a million trading shares on the Net. By ITV's Jonathan Maitland'.

Mr Samad was shaking his head. 'Very big risk. Very big risk,' he said. What's more, *Tonight* now want me to broadcast regular reports on how I'm doing: at first I was worried that people would find it too self-indulgent, but Jeff The Editor thinks it will be great; 'TV without a safety net,' he calls it. He reckons it's a good way of getting our viewers involved in two topics that television finds it hard to make interesting, i.e. the net and the stock market. So now, what started as an out-of-work-hours project has actually become my work. Truly, this thing has completely taken over my life.

Thursday, 20 April

18.00: All the world loves a loser. I'm getting e-mails from people offering me support, advice, condolence and share tips. I've even had one – from a bloke at www.laughingcock.com – asking me if he can superimpose my face over a pair of naked buttocks. The buttocks in question adorn the front page of his new gay porn website. 'It's going to be a fabulous growth area, Jonathan. Please let me do it. PS: I think I'm falling in love with you.'

What is remarkable – apart from all the money I've lost recently – is that e-mails are now coming in from all over the world: Australia, Russia, Sweden, Saudi Arabia, Denmark and, for some reason, Tonga. And the data shows that I'm getting several visitors from the United States Federal Justice Department.

Sally is back next weekend and has sent me an e-mail saying she's looking forward to reading the latest instalments of this book. No way, mate. On second thoughts I'll give her a dummy copy with all references to her edited out.

Saturday, 22 April

P.M.: Well, well. What a coincidence. Quite by chance I was introduced to Luke Johnson tonight – as in the City 'star' I read about in that *Private Eye* article. (The one that described how

Big Names In The City were making loads of dosh on the strength of being associated with new dotcom outfits.)

I was at a place called the Cobden in Notting Hill (one of those Clubs With Comfortable Sofas For Media Trendies) when the manager introduced us.

'I've just read a very interesting article about you,' I said as we shook hands. 'I'm writing a book about the stock market and it's come in very useful.'

He stiffened. 'You'd better be careful. I can just about ignore libels when they're in magazine form but if they're in a book, well, that's more permanent.'

I didn't want to libel him, I said, I wanted to interview him. So I am: in a couple of weeks.

PS: I think I may have graduated from being D-list celeb to the heady heights of a C. Previously, anyone who recognised me didn't actually know who I was or what I did. Now they still don't know my name, but they have some inkling of what I do. As I was walking away from the cashpoint this evening a young bloke ran in front of me, jogged backwards for a bit while studying my face, and then started shouting to his mate, 'Yeah, it is him, that one who's lost his house.'

Tuesday, 25 April

I am being dragged into the murky underworld of the stock market! Someone rang today and asked if I wanted 'in' on a pump 'n' dump. (I'd love to tell you who, but I can't. Revealing sources and all that.)

Pumping 'n' dumping, you will remember, is not what Peter Stringfellow types get up to in Ibiza, but cyberbanditry. Someone talks up a share big time on an Internet chat room (the pump) with the aim of selling it (the dump) once the price has gone up.

I agreed, but only to see how the thing works. To make money from it would be immoral, as I'd be misleading and defrauding fellow investors. But that hasn't stopped others; it is, in effect, what the City Slickers were doing. No one has been put in the clinker for it, though: if they were, it would be my good mates at the Financial Services Authority who would be putting them there. But so far – because it's so difficult and expensive to prove – the FSA are opting for education, not incarceration. Mind you, the DTI report into the Slickers' activities still hasn't been published: it may be that someone High Up will yet choose to make an example of them. I doubt it, though.

In America meanwhile, pumping-and-dumping has turned into big business: rumour has it that the Mafia are involved on a grand scale. In fact one bloke, who freely admits to being a professional p'n'd merchant, has made more than $7 million in the last two years. Tokyo Joe, as he calls himself, has a website. He fills it with racy, 'fill your boots' type stock market tips, and makes his money through subscription; more than 3,000 people pay more than $1,000 a year for his advice. (Work it out! $3,000 \times \$1,000 = \$3$ million a year!)

Tokyo is a flash git: on his website there are pictures of him with big cigars, fast cars, and gorgeous women. He calls himself 'a visionary', but the US Government, which is taking him to court on charges of corruption and misrepresentation, doesn't agree.

Tokyo argues that he is performing a useful social service; he says he is showing people the difference between fear and greed (the two things, as the old saying goes, that drive the stock market) and that anyone who follows his tips and gets burned only has themselves to blame. He reckons the government is abusing the right to free speech by trying to curtail his activities, and he plans to fight them all the way: it should be an interesting one.

The average UK pumper-and-dumper, if my experience is anything to go by, is a lot less glamorous than Tokyo. The ringleader of the operation, my contact told me, would be a bloke called 'Bob'.

Bob, he said, would be ringing me on Thursday morning at

precisely 11.15. He wouldn't talk openly about things: he would be using a strange code language. If I wanted 'in', I would have to give him certain set answers. Bob, I was told, would immediately ask for someone called 'Diana'. To which I was to reply, 'She's not in. She's gone down the shops to get some sausages and mash' (No, I'm not making this up). Bob would then say, 'You know where she should go, don't you?' My reply was to be: 'No. Tell me.'

Bob would then give the name of the company to be pumped and dumped, before ringing off, and I could then buy shares in that company, in advance of Bob and his pals plastering hype about it all over the Internet. The reason Bob was letting me in on things, my contact said, was because he'd been told (by my contact) that I was 'OK', and that I would return the favour by letting him in on future 'pumps' of my own.

So this is how it happens!

Thursday, 27 April

11.18: Bob is reliable if nothing else. He called on the dot of 11.15 and the conversation went exactly as scripted. He had a flat, monotone Essex accent, which for some reason I found myself mimicking: we sounded like one of those old Peter Cook and Dudley Moore head-to-head sketches.

The place to go for sausages and mash, he told me, was Action Computer Supplies. I've just checked their share price and it's £1.25. If Bob and his chums' little scam works out then it should soon be shooting up. I tried dialling 1471 to find out where he'd been ringing from but not surprisingly it didn't work.

17.00: Have checked loads of bulletin boards but there's nothing about Action Computer Supplies.

Friday, 28 April

Still no sign of Bob's cybergraffiti. I think he may have given up. Action's share price has actually dropped a few pence, and the market generally is pretty depressed. I reckon Bob has decided that what worked two months ago isn't going to now. Back then there were thousands of eager and gullible punters ready and willing to believe anything they read: the perfect conditions for a pump 'n' dumper. Now, thanks to the crash, they've all become more sceptical.

Truly, Bob is (was?) a creature of his time.

Saturday, 29 April

Sally got back today. She looked great. We avoided any personal stuff and talked a lot about golf – she'd started taking lessons out there. I felt a bit of a twinge when she told me how good-looking her coach was. Mind you, this could open some interesting avenues: we have arranged to play together, just her and me, some time soon.

Friday, 5 May

Surprise, surprise, I'm not going to sell my website for £5 million after all. I got a letter from John Sewell of Phase8 this morning saying that because of the crash all the company's plans have been put on hold for a few months. Oh well. I never took it seriously then, so I'm not even remotely disappointed now.

Mind you, the data for the website (showing a healthy 10,000 users a week) reveals that I'm still getting 'hit' from all over the world. That means I'm getting regular, intense interest on a global scale. I wonder what it would take for someone (with deep pockets and an even deeper belief in the power of the Internet) to decide that that kind of regular, global interest is worth buying up.

Then again, in a way they already have: Michael Lusada, the bloke from equitytracker.com I saw a few weeks ago, has offered me an interesting deal and I've accepted. He's putting an ad on my site and anyone who clicks through will be offered the chance to open an account with one of the (ever increasing) number of on-line brokers out there. Each time someone signs up this way,

I get a small cut of the commissions earned. I've done the sums: if 20 people a month get snaffled this way, it'll net me roughly £500 by the end of this year.

Which ain't gonna make me a million. On the other hand, if the Sultan of Brunei's son happened to log on and start spending freely, I might be in with a shout. But at least I have invested my site with that all-important quality which prospective buyers look for: 'value', i.e. something that's potentially worthless, but because you can't put an exact figure on it is also – potentially – very valuable indeed. (It all depends which way the wind's blowing.)

And thanks to an article in the *FT* by Alpesh Patel, whom I interviewed for my *Tonight* report ('What you're doing is *not* a strategy for widows and orphans, Jonathan, but as a journalistic experiment it's very brave and exciting and I admire you for it'), I've got another mega ad deal: Pearson, publishers of books about investment, are placing an advert on the site for a month, for £2,000.

My portolio may be looking a trifle sickly – it's recovered a bit, and is now hovering around the £52,000 mark – but I can at least lay claim to being one of the few dotcom ventures in Britain that is making a genuine cash profit.

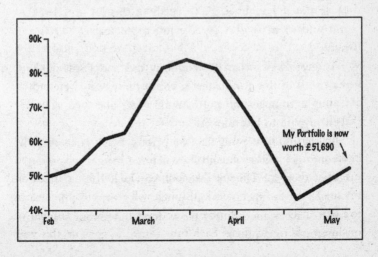

NAME OF CO.	INITIAL STAKE	SHARE PRICE THEN	SHARE PRICE NOW	WHAT'S MY STAKE WORTH NOW, THEN?
Autonomy 1	£30,000	£58.55	£69.30	£20,280*
Autonomy 2	£15,000	£102	£69.30	£10,140
Kewill	£10,000	£19.75	£12.42	£6,210
Oxygen	£2,500	25p	7p	£640
Charlton	£2,500	54p	54p	£2,500
Birchin	£2,500	12p	4p	£760
Airtel	£2,500	38p	29p	£1,860
Pace	£2,500	£11.09	£7.60	£1,680
Nike	£2,500	£18	£27.05	£3,750
Payforview (New!)	£3,500	30p	20p	£2,370
Cash Reserves	£1,500			£1,500
TOTAL				£51,690

*Taking into account £30,000 profits I took on Magic Thursday, i.e. allowing for deductions caused by 'Topslicing' as it's called.

As you can see, the line-up has changed a bit in the last couple of weeks: I have sold off three shares, for the following reasons:
1) 4Front. I bought £2,500 worth of this lot at £14.90 and sold them at £11.10. I've lost more than £700 as a result.

I never knew what this company did, and I still don't: the moral of the story is that if you're brave/stupid enough to buy a company on the basis that you like their name, then prepare to lose money.

In the unlikely event that the price actually goes up (as 4Front's did, quite substantially, when the market was going potty), then for Christ's sake sell: you will have a) made yourself an unexpected profit purely by acting like an arse and b) have a good dinner party story under your belt for some time to come.

2) just2clicks. Again, £2,500 worth, bought at £2.68. I got out at £1.20, losing nearly £1,400 in the process. Two lessons learned here: buying on day one of a public flotation is nearly always a Very Stupid Thing To Do Indeed. You won't lose anything by standing back for a few weeks, and letting the hullabaloo surrounding the launch die down.

Secondly: the much vaunted 'Business to Business' (B2B) cashfest that was supposed to happen, led by just2clicks, hasn't. Yet.

And even if it does, it won't be this year. Experts are now saying that B2B networks are indeed Good Things, and will change the way industry operates, but the real benefits will, for the most part, be passed on to the consumer. Good news, then, if you like buying new cars; bad news if, like me, you fell for the 'B2B will change the world' hype.

3) MV Sports: Again £2,500 worth, bought at 4p. I sold them at 1.5p, making myself a disastrous loss of more than £1,500. I am a twat: I should have sold the moment they fell to 3p. In fact I should also sell the other lame ducks in my pond, Birchin and Oxygen: but they would net me so little money I don't see the point.

The lesson to be learned here is that penny shares (i.e. ones of less than 50p) are *highly* speculative punts. For every story along the lines of 'I made a fortune out of a penny share' there are hundreds of untold ones in which the opposite happened. The fact is, if a share costs 1p, it's almost certainly because that's all it's worth.

As you can see, I have used what money I have left from these three investments to buy £3,500 worth of shares in a company called PayForView.

It's a bit like taking the rubble from three houses destroyed by a storm and using it to build a new one.

Mind you, this new house is built on similarly shaky foundations: it's a highly speculative punt on a hi-tech US outfit that specialises in putting content on the Internet (TV programmes, films, etc.) and charging people to download it. If I was a sensible investor I wouldn't go near this lot: but I am still determined to make as much money as possible on the basis that you only get high returns if you take high risks. And what's more, my mate Alpesh from the *FT* says this lot might – might – have it in them to go up tenfold, soon. We shall see.

Monday, 8 May

I met Luke Johnson – star City player – today. We chatted over coffee near his office, just off Bond Street. He bought the coffees, but then so he should: according to the *Sunday Times* Rich List he is worth £80 million. (Mind you, he says their figures are way off.)

He was a lot less defensive than when I met him at the Cobden Club: he was clearly satisfied that I wouldn't repeat the (according to him) potentially libellous stuff that's been written about him in publications like *Private Eye* and the *Guardian*. I asked him what motivated those kind of reports. He reckoned it had something to do with his father, Paul Johnson: the famous right-wing ranter who writes scathing articles (e.g. how the country is falling apart because of porn on Channel 5) to order for the *Daily Mail*.

Are his critics jealous of him? 'That describes emotions of a sexual nature . . . I'd rather use the term envy.' If people on the *Guardian* hate capitalism – which they clearly do, he said – then they shouldn't become financial journalists: they should stick to current affairs and politics.

He also said one thing that reminded me of something that worried me a few months back: it's all very well betting the farm on one hi-tech company, he explained, but the hi-tech world moves frighteningly fast. If someone from Silicon Valley suddenly springs up with a bigger, better and cheaper way of doing things, then the company you've bunged the lot on will be dead in the water. Overnight. Eek. I drifted off for a couple of minutes after that, visualising the horrible possibility of a mini, bearded American version of Mike Lynch appearing out of nowhere.

What about the implication that it may have been somehow improper for him to have profited so much from Blake's Clothing suddenly turning itself into a groovy e-commerce outfit?

No way, said Mr Johnson. He wasn't a director of the company, he just held shares in it. If he'd had a seat on the board, then he would have felt a moral responsibility not to have cashed in. But, he said, it wasn't his idea to make Blake's change its clothes, as it were: the press just painted it that way. His involvement was merely a coincidence, which was seized on by certain sections of the press as evidence of something more. There wasn't much he could do, he said: he only cashed in soon afterwards because it was clear to him that Internet share prices were unfeasibly high.

We said goodbye and he wished me good luck. In the cab I reflected on what he'd told me. Luke Johnson, it seemed to me, was a man 'guilty' of only one thing: making money out of his reputation. And what's wrong with that?

Thursday, 11 May
I've been checking on all those day traders I interviewed earlier this year: the ones who were coining it.

Not surprisingly they now have a very different story to tell.

Roger Pritchard, the singer from the Brotherhood of Man, sounded more chirpy than he had any right to be, given that in the last few weeks he's lost, on paper — wait for it — more than £100,000. (Then again he's used to controlling his emotions: he's had to sing 'Save Your Kisses For Me' more than 3,000 times, without breaking down in tears.)

'Oh no, I'm not worried,' he said. 'I've been doing this for fourteen years now and I've never failed to make a profit.'

Roger starts each year with a massive lump sum – this year it was roughly £500,000 – which he then uses to play the markets. 'Come the end of the year I know I'll be back in profit,' he said, in a strange, soothing way – part *Jackanory*, part friendly GP. 'My worst year ever was 1993, and even then I made money, four per cent growth it was.'

Sally Mitchell, the world-famous dog prints woman, has had an even worse time. When I met her earlier this year she wouldn't tell me how much profit she'd made, but now she was prepared to give details. Back then she was £350,000 (!) up – on paper. Now she's lost it. All of it. More than a third of a million down the pan in a matter of weeks. She is now back where she started.

'What a bloody fool I was not selling,' she said.

Then again, Sally and Roger are two very well-off individuals: it might be painful losing such huge sums, but they are playing with money they can afford to lose. Lucky them.

One bloke has e-mailed me with a sorry tale of money that he couldn't afford to lose. His name is Paul Bell, and he has lost his life savings. All £23,000 of them. Gone. Paul is 39 (same as me: eek . . . bad omen) and is a professional gambler. But not a very good one. He got sucked into the stock market, like me, after reading countless stories about people making millions out of hi-tech shares. He put £15,000 into a telecoms company and everything was going fine until one day last month, when the company announced it was hiving off part of its operations, to form a separate outfit.

Unfortunately the bit being hived off was, by general consent, deemed to be the best bit. It was rather like Manchester United announcing the sale of their entire first team, apart from the Neville brothers. One day last month poor old Paul logged on and saw his company do the stock market equivalent of letting the air out of a large balloon, very quickly. He was losing money, at one stage, 'at the rate of roughly a hundred pounds every thirty seconds'. He was terrified. He turned white. 'I'd never seen myself turning white before,' he told me, in a friendly Yorkshire accent. (By now e-mail had turned to phone.) But what made things uncontrollably horrific was that his on-line brokers didn't deal in that particular share: he had had to phone a traditional stock-broker in order to buy it. And so he had to use the phone to sell it, too. The trouble was, that particular stockbroker had only a handful of phone lines, but hundreds of people in the same boat as Paul. So Paul spent most of the day in question on the phone, listening to an engaged tone, while the blood drained from his face and the money drained from his bank account. Unfortunately he'd actually borrowed money as well: and so the next day, in order to clear his debt, he found himself having to sell his car: 'Top-of-the-range Hyundai coupé, cost me twenty thousand, had to sell it for eight thousand, coz I needed the money quick, y'see. Broke my heart.' He never told his fiancée about all this: he still hasn't. I hope she's not reading this. But he has, at least, income still coming in: he is the voice of Channel 4 Racing's telephone hotline service, which gives out hot horse-racing tips every day.

And that is why he's got in touch. He wants to challenge me to a 'million-pound duel': he thinks he can earn a million pounds, betting on the horses, faster than I can, on the stock market.

He will also be using £50,000: not his own money, mind you – he's found people in the betting industry to back him. He wants me to mention his project on my website, and he'll do the same in return. I don't see why not: it should 'drive traffic to my site', as we say in the Internet business, i.e. make more people visit my cyberpremises. That in turn will be good for my 'hit rate' (currently running at a healthy 70,000 a week) which, in turn, will be good for attracting potential advertisers. My God! I'm talking like a businessman!

Friday, 12 May

Wonderful news. The cricket season is upon us. Me and my mates have run a team for the last 12 years (I've never missed a match in all that time) and the first game of the season is on Sunday. I keep ringing up the long-range weather forecast to check on the likely conditions. Having a bat in your hand, waiting at the wicket, while a bowler runs up, ready to hurl the ball at you, is probably the most all-consuming thing there is. Even during sex you might think, momentarily, of something (or even somebody) else: but with cricket you can't afford to let your mind wander for a moment. And if you get to smack the ball to the boundary (not a feeling I'm overly familiar with), OK, it's not quite as good as sex: but my God it's satisfying.

Monday, 15 May

Shit. I got five runs. They were good ones, mind you.

Wednesday, 17 May

First we had the 'Everyone's Making Money Out Of The Net' articles: now we're getting the 'What Went Wrong' follow-ups.

The most convincing explanation I've yet read can be summed up like this: it was all down to Irrational Exuberance fuelled by a) media hype, b) the onset of the new millennium and c) hopelessly optimistic predictions of how much new wealth the Internet could generate.

Warren Buffett, the 'Investment Guru' who's made more money than virtually any other investor in the world (we're talking billions), has never had any truck with Internet stocks and shares, because, he says, he 'doesn't understand them'. His is beginning to look like quite a wise decision. He compares the Net to aeroplanes: they have fundamentally changed the world, and the way we live, but the profits to be made out of them have never been that high because there's always been so much competition.

I wish I'd thought of that.

Friday, 19 May

Oh dear. Turned on the *Today* prog this morning and heard what sounded like a requiem Mass for hi-tech shares.

boo.com (purveyors of adverts that were so busy being hip they forgot to tell you what the company actually did, i.e. sell clothes over the Net) have gone bust.

My portfolio is back in the sick bay: back down to less than 50k. It's a bit unfair: despite what Warren Buffett says, dismissing the Internet's prospects just because one firm has gone under is a bit like saying no one is going to eat meat any more, just because the local high-street butcher has closed down.

But it's all to do with sentiment: and the doom-mongers are having their day once more.

boo.com, like Lastminute, were, arguably, victims of their own hype.

They were run by two Scandinavians, a gorgeous blonde and a handsome brown-haired geezer, so publicity – and lots of money from willing venture capitalists – was never hard to come by. Fortunately, boo wasn't quoted on the stock market so no small private investors got burned. But alas, many small investors in other high-profile hi-techs have been. Step forward Paul Bell.

The big question is, who's to blame? Us? For swallowing the hype?

Well, up to a point, yes, Lord Copper.

The events of the last few months have highlighted the risks of following the advice of 'star analysts' who say, 'Buy these shares, they're great.'

Let me give you an example: when Lastminute.com (sorry, them again) was about to come to market, one expert kept getting quoted. Her name was Mary Meeker. Mary Meeker of Morgan Stanley Dean Witter, that is – the hugely respected and highly influential investment bank. A typical Mary quote was that the company had 'great worldwide potential'. The inference seemed to be clear: Mary's an expert. She thinks the company's great. You should think seriously about buying into it.

There was only one problem, though, which few pointed out at the time, but which seemed pretty obvious to anyone who looked beneath the surface. The bank handling Lastminute's flotation – and therefore in a perfect position to benefit from it, if it went well – was (wait for it) Morgan Stanley Dean Witter.

That's right. The very people Mary Meeker worked for.

Mary has done nothing wrong, least of all in the legal sense – but it is a clear example of the kinds of conflict of interest that have been around in the City for ages. And it's certainly not Last-minute's fault, either: they seem to be getting dragged out to sea by currents beyond their control.

This is something I shall have to talk about with – hallelujah! – Mike Lynch. At last, he has agreed to see me: I'm going up to Cambridge for a chat next week.

Tuesday, 23 May

Today I met Mike Lynch. He was much smaller than I thought he'd be. And the beard looked neater than it did in photos.

I wanted to ask him about it the moment he walked through the door, but I made myself hold off just in case. I didn't know the bloke . . . what if he had a Sense Of Humour Failure?

He didn't walk in, actually, he sauntered. And smiled. He was all casual – chinos and open-necked shirt.

'It's not *really* true, is it? You haven't really mortgaged your house, have you?'

Yup.

'Hasn't anyone told you about portfolio diversification?'

Don't start telling me that now, I said. I asked him a question.

Does it worry you, knowing there are people like me, whose fortunes are riding on your back?

'God, yes. I think about it every day. I shouldn't be doing this job if I didn't. I get letters from little old grannies in Leicestershire thanking me, which is great, but when I get letters like I did the other day, from a bloke saying "Thank you! I am never *ever* selling these shares!" I get really worried.'

I wanted to ask him there and then whether I should sell – but I couldn't: the law forbids him from giving information which might affect his own share price. OK, then. How did it all start? From nothing to a two billion company, in less than 10 years?

Answer: in a pub.

He had the idea for Autonomy in the early 90s but couldn't get anyone to back him. Then he met an old bloke in a pub, told him all about it, and got a £6,000 loan. He's lost touch with the old bloke since.

Sounds like a made-up PR story, I said.

'Absolutely not.' (If the old bloke is reading this, I suggest he gets in touch: Autonomy is now worth £3 billion.)

Mike's personal fortune is estimated at £600 million. What does he do with it?

'Not much . . . I haven't got the time.'

He's not one for flash cars and cigars, our Mike: he's more Bill Gates than Larry Ellison. He spends a few hundred quid on exotic fish every so often and bungs the rest of his dosh in his local bank account.

High-interest account?

'No. I do absolutely nothing with it. Indefensible money management, I know, but there we go.'

Something else worried me. Every three months, he takes 20 million quid out of the company: i.e. he sells some of his shares. Hardly a good sign for shareholders like me if the CEO is selling at that rate, I said.

'I do it regularly so that no one's surprised by it,' he said. 'If I sold a huge amount as a one-off, it might get people panicking. But if everyone knows what I'm doing, in advance, then that's less likely to happen.'

I was a little bit worried by that – I mean, he hardly *needs* to take 20 million out every quarter, does he? But then again, why shouldn't he? I let it pass.

Mike is . . . well, normal. Halfway through the chat his mobile went off. He popped out of the room and I could hear him laughing uproariously.

'Personal or professional?' I asked him when he came back in.

'Bit of both.'

You'd have thought Mike spent his university years (he went to Cambridge, natch) chained to a desk in the college library, but no. There was an awful lot of drinking, chasing women, and – good sign, this – music: he played sax with a band called Fast Joe and The Accelerators.

'I never got up until twelve: I had a good time. I could have worked non-stop but what good would that have done? There's a limit to how much the human mind can take in. I was always interested by the idea of using technology to fill in the gap between what the human mind can and can't achieve.' Hence Autonomy, I thought.

But how does a bloke from Essex (his brother is a builder; they get on great, he said) get to conquer the City? Didn't he get intimidated by all those posh public school types who must have looked down their noses at him?

'No. I learnt how to deal with them pretty early on. I went to a posh school myself – I got a scholarship – and there were two types of kids there: posh thick ones and the bright scholarship kids. It didn't take us long to work things out. We ran the place. The City can be a bit like that, so it wasn't hard to deal with.'

OK, the time had come. The Beard question. I eased my way

in. Martha Lane Fox, I said. No beard, lots of hype. It's rebounded on her. You: beard. Less hype, more success. Has it helped?

'Are you suggesting she's more attractive than me?'

No . . . but image is important, isn't it? And beards says certain things to certain people.

Silence. More Silence. Then:

'Actually, it helped. When I first went to the City as a clean-shaven twentysomething, no one took me seriously. I looked too young. When I grew this [he pointed to the bush on his chin] they were a lot more forthcoming – it made me look trust-worthy, so . . . yes, it has helped a lot.'

Aha! So you agree with Beard Investment Theory?

'Put it this way. I would tend to ask a lot more questions of a chief executive without a beard than one with.'

But that's not to decry the Lastminute high-octane publicity approach, he said; there are three ways to create a buzz in the City, and that's one of them. Trouble is, it can rebound on you. A woman in America, the CEO of a big dotcom, recently posed for a glossy magazine in a black cocktail dress and it put investors right off: wrong image.

So what are the other two ways to get the City interested, and money pouring in?

'Well . . . build a really good solid business based on a really good idea . . . boring. I know.'

The third?

'The Squiffy method.'

Squiffy?

'Yeah. Brokers' whispers. Get all your posh mates in the City to take their posh mates into the corridor and whisper things like "Squiffy says this company is damned good. Buy". Which is not good. The whole thing is built on rumour and that's not healthy at all.'

Hmmm. Time to go. We shook hands. By the way . . . I'm in

a band, I said. Surf 'n' Turf. Fancy them for the Autonomy Christmas party?

He said he'd think about it.

My defining thought came in the taxi on the way to Cambridge station.

You can have all the investment theories in the world but – here comes a cliché – when it comes down to it, it's all about investing in people.

I genuinely liked Mike Lynch, and felt I could trust him: I think my money is safe.

Tuesday, 30 May

Oh boy. Sally has started going out with someone.

She met him playing tennis at the Harbour Club and he's been doing the red roses and weekends in Paris routine. She broke the news to me gently . . . she didn't actually say the words 'going out' (deliberately, I think) but I know that's what's happened. He only frigging stayed the night earlier this week. He sounds appalling.

Thursday, 1 June

11.00: Oh God. I met him this evening. We all sat round the table at the Harbour Club and I tried to be nice to him but there wasn't a great deal of chemistry between us. He's posh, in his early 40s, and his name's Edward. And he's a stiff. Halfway through the meal I realised I disliked him intensely. Sally says he's a 'rilly decent person, Jahnathan', but who cares? I hate him.

Saturday, 3 June

Hurrah. Another cricket game. Something to take my mind off the two things that have taken me over. We won: I got two runs. Good ones, mind you.

Sunday, 4 June

My portfolio has spent the last two months edging up and then retreating again. Overall, things have improved significantly since my flirtation with oblivion in mid-April: my original £50k is now worth roughly £62k. That represents an annual rate of return of nearly 30%: a hell of a lot better than the so-called 'professionals' in the City manage, most years.

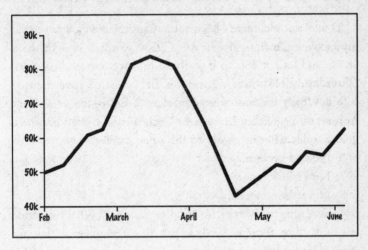

NAME OF CO.	INITIAL STAKE	SHARE PRICE THEN	SHARE PRICE NOW	WHAT'S MY STAKE WORTH NOW, THEN?
Autonomy 1	£30,000	£58.55	£95.20	£28,220*
Autonomy 2	£15,000	£102	£95.20	£14,110
Kewill	£10,000	£19.75	£9.42	£4,710
Oxygen	£2,500	25p	7p	£640
Birchin	£2,500	12p	4p	£760
Airtel	£2,500	38p	31p	£1,980
Pace	£2,500	£11.09	£9.04	£1,995

Nike	£2,500	£18	£27.24	£3,770
PayForView	£3,500	30p	20p	£2,370
Vocalis (new!)	£2,500	£2.33	£2.33	£2,500
Cash Reserves	£1,500			£1,500
TOTAL				£62,555

* Figure includes £30,000 of profits I cashed in on Magic Thursday

As you can see, there's been some transfer activity. I have sold my beloved Charlton shares. All £2,500 worth. I bought them at 54p and sold at 55p, so if you take into account dealing costs, I have made No Profit Whatsoever. But at least I haven't made a loss. Which reminds me of a story I heard the other day. Apparently Legendary Investment Guru Warren Buffett has three golden rules when it comes to the stock market:

1) Never lose money.
2) Never lose money.
3) Never lose money.

So according to Warren, no less, I've done OK. What happened with Charlton, though? Well, as you may remember, I thought their price would rise as punters realised they were headed for the riches of the Premier League (more TV money, bigger gates, etc.). And indeed it did: to 65p. But then once they got promoted, everyone realised that they would probably go straight back down again. So they sold.

I had two choices: wait for the new season, and hope Charlton get off to a blinder, in which case 100p would be realistic, or sell now and put the dosh on something else.

It wasn't a hard one: I've followed Charlton for 33 years.

The money from the sale has been bunged on . . .

Vocalis

They specialise in voice technology gadgets . . . i.e. sending voice messages over the Net, voice-activated gizmos, etc. Yup . . .

hi-tech again. What I like about them is that they're spending loads on research and development, and are a lot lower now (£2.33) than they were at the height of The Madness.

The trouble is, my million still seems rather a long way off. There is one way to make a *lot* of money very quickly, though . . . but I said I'd never do it again.

Monday, 5 June

M3200 – I can't get it out of my mind. M3200. That was the account number on my spread betting membership card. OK, I know I destroyed it and said never again but for some reason the thought doesn't seem as unacceptable as it once did: the terror of that Monday when I lost 8k on Autonomy has healed.

I can't be that unlucky twice, surely?

The thing is, I keep seeing shares whose values have gone up, say, a quid in a week. And I can't stop thinking. If I'd had £50 a penny on that, I'd have made five grand. Or £100 a penny . . . ten grand!

It's that 'high risk, high reward' thing: take the former and you're in with a chance of the latter.

Tuesday, 6 June

Fuck it, I'm going for it. I am going to do a spread bet. On the Techmark. The Techmark is an index, quoted in points: at the moment it's at about 3,500. It represents the combined value of top hi-tech shares on the London Stock Exchange. I reckon it's going down.

Why? Because some of the big guns in hi-tech land – Kingston, Baltimore and Psion – are losing ground fast. In fact it looks like they'll be heading *out* of the all-important FOOTSIE Top 100, very soon.

When that happens – as I said earlier – the mega-huge FOOTSIE 100 'tracker funds' that do nothing but stock up big time on those 100 companies will have to sell them.

I reckon a lot of people will be selling in advance of that selling, if you see what I mean: so I'm bunging £50 a point on the Techmark going down.

Thursday, 8 June

11.22: Have just rung my mate Mark in the City. Glory be. The Techmark is down. Big Time. I have closed the bet and made £3,250. Fortune favours the brave.

The irony is the Techmark went down for completely different reasons from the ones I foresaw: something to do with interest rates in America. But hey: who cares!

Tuesday, 13 June

OK. Time to recoup the rest of my spread betting losses.

I've placed four:

1) BskyB to go down (lots of uncertainty over whether they'll get the rights to screen live soccer on TV: the City hates uncertainty).

2) Baltimore, a hi-tech biggie, to go down: see Index Tracker theory.

3) Bookham, another hi-tech biggie, to go up: again, Index Tracker theory, but in reverse; it's about to join the top 100.

4) Scoot.com, an Internet stock, to go down. I've been following its progress recently and it's just reached a high: I feel it will fall at the end of this week.

Thursday, 15 June

12.00: Oh dear. British Sky Broadcasting won the TV footie contract, and paid less for it than the experts feared. Their share price has rocketed. I had a controlled-risk bet in place so lost £1,600 – but that's all – straight away. On the plus side, Scoot.com is indeed falling and Bookham is edging up to £37.45 – the point at which I start coining it.

17.00: Bit worrying. Bookham has taken a nosedive. It is close of play and it's fallen two quid since I last looked. I am four grand down.

Friday, 16 June

09.00: Jesus Christ, it's happening again. The red arrow pointing downwards next to Bookham has 2.80 next to it . . . it's fallen another 280p this morning.

Oh God: I can ring and ask the spread betting company what my position is or hold and be strong. I'm going to be strong.

09.04: No I'm not. It's still a long way down from here. I've closed out. And lost another eight grand. I am walking around my front room in circles in my pyjamas feeling scared and sick. Again.

16.25: Small consolation: Scoot has netted me a grand, but Baltimore hasn't budged and I didn't fancy another rout so I closed the bet and lost £500 on it.

22.00: I am trying to be philosophical about it: I have now lost £14,000 in total on spread betting. Fourteen thousand pounds. Fourteen thousand pounds.

But the website is earning me plenty and there's always the £15,000 I got for this book, so it's not as bad as it sounds. Maybe I should have held on to Bookham?

Tuesday, 20 June

Yeah. Maybe I should. It's now cruised to well over £40: if I hadn't panicked, I would be 4k up on that single bet, instead of 8k down. I can't stop thinking about it. I've been recording *House of Horrors*, my show about dodgy builders, this week but my mind is filled with figures all the time, even when I'm having conversations with people. ('If I put a hundred quid a penny on it and it goes up . . .'). It's there in my head and I can't get rid of it: I'm more obsessed than I've ever been. I'm not addicted, am I?

Friday, 23 June

It's the excitement that's doing it. You know that feeling you get when someone asks you what you'd do if you won the lottery, and for one glorious split second your imagination fools you into experiencing the sensation that you have? You know: sudden, genuine euphoria.

Well, what I keep getting – and can't escape from – is a bit like that, except it's more compelling because the prospect of it coming true is so much more real. The odds on winning the lottery are one in several million: the odds on a share going up substantially in the course of a year are much, much lower. The key words here are 'in the course of a year' . . . so far, I've been panicked into selling the moment something's gone wrong. Had I waited, I wouldn't be in the position I am now.

If only I'd conquered my fear.

Now, I am going to – I think.

A plan is developing in my head; I am going to go for the shit-or-bust option. I am going to back four companies that I've been following closely, big time, to go up by the end of the year.

At some point between now and then they are *bound* to hit considerably higher levels. The only problem will be ignoring them if (and when) they go down. I must *not* be panicked into selling: even if it means clearing out my current account completely, to keep the bets up and running.

What if it goes wrong? Well . . . if it goes wrong, I've worked out that the maximum I can lose is . . . £150,000.

But that's not going to happen. And even if it did, the value of my house (it's gone up a lot since I bought it 10 years ago) should just about cover it.

And that is taking into account the 50k mortgage that I took out to start this whole thing off.

I'm in it up to my neck.

I could always move in with Richard (Normal), I suppose.

But the upside is this: if the shares hit anything like the heights I think they will, I'll be looking at anything up to 100 grand of pure tax-free profit. Maybe more. I've just got to conquer the fear. I'll think about it over the weekend and then take a decision on Monday. I'm not being stupid: just brave.

Saturday, 24 June

In the US, Amazon, the flagship Internet stock – one of the big ones, by which the whole sector is judged – fell by 20% yesterday: I wonder if that will spark off yet another slump? Three of the four firms I'm thinking of betting on big time are hi-tech, so I'd better wait till the US markets are well and truly open on Monday afternoon at the very earliest before committing myself for the third (and, whichever way it turns out, final) time. I'll wait and see.

Four words: high risk, high reward.

Monday, 26 June

Amazon shares are getting slaughtered. One top analyst, who's been a massive backer of the company for ages, has even said she's 'throwing in the towel'. Not the best time to be indulging in spread bets on hi-tech companies, then.

Monday, 3 July

Now is the time to go for it. On Friday night I was a guest on Sky TV, on their *Business Report* programme. My fellow guest was a stockbroker called Tony Craze who's made a bit of a name for himself as a media pundit. It's easy to see why. He is big, grey-haired, in his late 40s, and doesn't talk Impenetrable Stock Market Jargon Babble in an off-putting upper-class accent.

He chats calmly and reassuringly about shares, a bit like a grown-up version of the Paul Whitehouse 'Geezer' character from *The Fast Show*, the one who says 'I'm a little bit woo, a little bit whuurrr'.

He has a nice, inclusive Everyman approach: shares aren't 'over-priced', they're 'a little bit warm, a little bit toppy'.

Tony reckons Sopheon, a firm involved in the field of 'knowledge management', are destined for big things by the end of the year. They are currently around £4.50: some experts reckon they could go to £23. Tony thinks that's 'a bit warm, a bit toppy', but feels £12 is well within reach. Apparently they are due to get official approval in the USA soon, for a mega partnership deal they've signed. When (if?) that comes, there should be a string of lucrative deals to follow, as a result. We shall see.

('Knowledge management' is in fact the same field that Autonomy are involved in, so I hope they're not destined for too great things.)

So: a potential triumph/disaster spread bet on Sopheon is in place. As indeed is another one on Autonomy – well, you've got to believe, haven't you? The other two are Independent Energy and Geo Interactive Media. Independent Energy is an independent supplier of energy (funny, that) to people in the Midlands. Earlier this year their share price was £33: it's now £5.50. The collapse has been caused by 'billing problems', i.e. customers are getting the wrong bills at the wrong time so there are big cash flow problems. But they are trying to sort things out and when they do . . . watch the price rocket. And let's face it, electricity isn't in danger of going out of fashion in the next few months, is it? (It is, as the saying goes, 'a defensive stock' – like water and gas shares.)

Geo, meanwhile, are an Israeli company who, like Independent Energy and Sopheon, are languishing massively below their high-tide marks for the year. Geo lead the field in putting video images on the Net and on mobile phones. Soon, you won't just hear the person you're ringing, you'll see them too. When that happens Geo will be the ones cashing in. And, I have to say, I have yet again been influenced by what I've read in the papers, even though I know I shouldn't be: one commentator wrote the other day, 'With some stocks it's hard to see where the income is going to come from: not so with Geo. The current price of £14.50 may well represent the last affordable chance for investors to scramble aboard.'

The potential problem about seeing opinions like that in print is that the very fact they are in print gives them a credibility they may well not deserve. But, hell – the seed has been planted in my brain and I can't stop it growing.

Thursday, 6 July

Hmm. I didn't think the first test of nerve would come so soon.

Two of the mega spread bets are going calamitously wrong. Geo Interactive Media have been slipping all week but now the directors have come out with the worst of all possible announcements: they're selling a bucketload of shares. They tried, in a statement, to pacify investors but it hasn't worked: Geo shares are about as popular as bacon sandwiches at a bar mitzvah.

In fact they've dropped 10%. That might not sound a lot to you but it means I'm currently more than £20,000 down on that one bet alone. However, I promised myself when I took it out that I wouldn't panic if this happened: so I'm not going to. I'm going to hang on in and pray that it rebounds by the end of the year.

The trouble is, the spread betting blokes keep phoning me and asking for huge cheques, just to keep the bet up and running: 'margin calls', they're called. So far I've already sent them £30,000, and the way things are going, I'm going to have to send them another £30,000. Trouble is, it's money I don't have. These are my options:

1) Ask the bank for a massive overdraft and tell them it's to pay off a tax bill.

2) Borrow the money off friends: I've already raised the spectre with Richard (Normal) but he didn't sound too impressed. Not surprising, really.

3) Sell the entire portfolio of shares.

4) I have a two-bedroomed flat in Epsom, in Surrey, which I bought two years ago, as an investment. It's my pension, basically. I could sell that for about £130,000: or so my estate agent told me, when I called him 20 minutes ago.

I never thought it would come to this: the only feeling I've ever had to compare with this was when my girlfriend told me, all those years ago, that she'd had it off with a French waiter in the South of France. It's a horrible, evil, deadening, sick-in-the-stomach kind of feeling.

The worst thing about it isn't the money itself – it is only money, after all, and I haven't closed the bet yet, so it's still only a paper loss – but the complete lack of control that I have over the situation.

I am a walking advert for Hamlet cigars. Come to think of it, maybe I should ask them if they want to sponsor my website.

I also wonder if I should seek professional help . . . Gamblers Anonymous. I don't think I will, though. I don't think I have a problem with gambling, I'm not addicted to it: I'm just not very good at it.

This particular cloud has one almighty black lining to it as well: Sally. I can't stop myself harbouring hopes that she still might go out with me, but when we got into a discussion yesterday about relationships she said – laughingly – how she could never go out with someone like me because I was – quote – 'too much of a project'. I think that's American shorthand for 'you're a thirty-nine-year-old bachelor weirdo with strange, ingrained personal habits which I couldn't put up with'. I pretended to laugh along with her but I felt it bad in my solar plexus.

Great, isn't it? I'm scared and I'm lonely. What a cocktail.

Friday, 7 July

It seems almost irrelevant to be showing you a graph of how the shares in my portfolio are doing, but here goes.

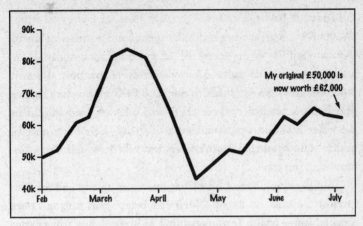

My original £50,000 is now worth £62,000

As you can see, I've been stuck in the corridor between £52k and £65k for months now. But it might turn out to be irrelevant, because the Spread Betting Thing could render the whole portfolio pretty much academic.

Looking relatively secure but it all depends on impending storm clouds

Impending storm cloud, from the spread betting continent: could destroy my house in seconds or (hopefully) dissipate, allowing sun to blaze freely

Sunday, 9 July

00.00: What a great weekend. Sally spent large portions of it with Edward Stiff; I spent nearly all of it alone, contemplating my imminent financial ruin. All my friends (apart from Richard Normal) are married with kids now, and I felt a bit uneasy ringing them to ask what they were up to and whether I could join in. Let's face it: the answer would almost certainly have been 'nothing much', and even if it hadn't been I would have felt like I was imposing anyway.

So self-pitying have I been that I've taken to my bed for long periods of time: some of which has been spent staring at the ceiling, some trying (unsuccessfully) to sleep. I held off ringing Richard (Normal) till this evening as going round to his place would have felt like an admission of defeat: but in the end I couldn't bear being on my own in my shitty maisonette any more, so I went round to his place for a game of Scrabble. What a glamorous, dangerous life I lead.

Monday, 10 July

I think I've now learned one thing after the horrendous spread betting episodes of the last few weeks: How To Live With Huge Paper Losses. When my bets on Bookham and Autonomy started to capsize I got scared, jumped out of the lifeboat and drowned. Had I stayed on board the storm would have passed and I could have floated serenely into the harbour waving at the crowds.

This time, at least, I am staying put: even though I am now facing a staggering £25,000 loss on my Autonomy and Geo Interactive Media bets. But having been here before I am used to the conditions. 'It is,' I keep telling myself, 'only a loss on paper.'

Mind you, I'm not sure whether my new-found calmness is a good thing or not.

I have at least managed to avoid selling my flat and raiding my pension fund, Robert Maxwell-style, in order to keep my debtors at bay.

I've had yet another letter from my spread betting company asking for several thousand quid, but fortunately my bank has fallen for the tax bill story and given me an overdraft facility of £50,000.

Wednesday, 12 July

Played golf first thing in the morning with Sally. She's certainly not one for fading into the background. She was wearing a tight pair of grey shorts which showed off her mouth-watering caramel thighs marvellously. I don't think I've ever enjoyed a game quite as much, in fact.

Mind you, even if she'd been wearing sackcloth and ashes she would have stood out. Being loud and competitive and American, she screams when she hits a bad shot (which is quite often as she's a beginner).

Marvellously, a little bit of dissatisfaction seems to be creeping in with Edward The Stiff. She is troubled by his more-often-than-is-necessary references to his ex-girlfriend.

I tried to slag him off, subtly.

'I don't think he appreciates you, Sally. You need someone who adores you and wants to look after you, and I know this is a terrible thing to say but maybe he doesn't.' All of a sudden I thought about adding the words 'but I do'. But I didn't. I was too scared.

Thursday, 13 July

Maybe I have learned something after all: my reading of Independent Energy's prospects appears to have been correct. When I took a spread bet out on them they were £5.50p. Now they're more than £8 and I'm £9,000 up – on paper.

I'm not going to make the same mistake as last time, when I

turned down the chance of making £6,000 on Autonomy: I've rung up my betting company and told them to close the bet the moment it falls below £6,000.

What's interesting here is that I have at last managed to predict something correctly *before* the experts: money has been pouring into Independent Energy all week for precisely the reasons I thought it might; they've also helped things along by announcing that they're thinking of building a new power station. Clearly, the City boys are thinking that if they're planning that, they can't be in too bad a position.

I've also learned something else: and that is the Huge Importance Of News Flow. In fact it's so important it's probably the single most crucial thing in keeping a company's share price buoyant/rising.

This is why: markets like good news. The more a company puts it out, the more people will buy it. The opposite is also true, of course: if a company announces less than expected profits, or that its main product causes cancer, no one's going to be filling their shopping trolleys with it.

But there's an art to announcing good news: if you have, say, three great things to announce and you let them all out at once, you've got nothing in the locker for the next few weeks. The share price might shoot up quickly but then fall back sharply as people take profits. But if the company establishes a policy of drip-feeding the markets with good news – i.e. staggers the stories, deliberately – it will help keep the share price up there. Especially if they actually let the market know that's what's going to happen, by announcing something like 'In the coming months we will regularly be announcing new orders'.

Mind you, they had better keep to their word: if they don't come up with the orders their price will start tailing off dramatically and they will get a reputation for being unreliable.

Another thing I've learned is how companies can protect

their share price by what's called 'Good Investor Relations'.

Let me give you an example. I met Tony Craze ('bit warm, bit toppy') for a cup of tea today, at his London offices. He has several multimillion-pound clients and has made them all a tidy profit. He is important. Important enough for his words to be dissected by stock market anoraks (like me) in Internet chat rooms.

He is, and always has been, a big fan of Baltimore Technologies, who are market leaders in Internet security products, and one of the standard-bearers for the new economy. (I really wish I'd met him earlier: he was singing the company's praises big time when they were just £5 a share. Months later they were £132. If I'd given Tony £40,000 – what I've spent on Autonomy this year, in fact – I would have cleared my million pounds comfortably by now and would be writing this not in my crappy front room in SW11 but in the Bahamas, sipping a Long Island iced tea and telling my caddy to polish the golf clubs.)

But anyway, the point is that Tony (who's an ex-boxer, by the way: surely the only boxer-turned-stockbroker in the world) told me that recently Baltimore had been having 'wobbles': in fact in just one day last week, they fell by a whopping 8%. Tony, who had a fair old wodge of his clients' money invested in the company, was, naturally, worried.

He could have panicked, but he took the decision that the fall didn't mean that there was a serious problem with the company, and that he should bail out: on the contrary. His reasoning was this. The fall in the share price had been caused by less than brill-iant profit announcements from two of Baltimore's competitors: the City lemmings assumed that meant bad news for the Internet security industry as a whole, and sold big time.

But Tony reckoned the competitors' poison was Baltimore's meat: their poor figures were simply down to the fact that Baltimore was doing better than they were, and winning more business.

But he wanted to check with the top dog at Baltimore, Fran

Rooney, first. So he called him. And because Baltimore are good at 'investor relations', Fran was happy a) to take the call, and also b) to give Tony an honest assessment of the situation, using only information that was readily available to the public. End result: Tony didn't panic and didn't sell. In fact he took advantage of the fall in price to buy more shares. Several million quids' worth. He also went on places like Sky TV and the Money Channel and told everyone watching (not a significant audience, but an influential one) that Baltimore were a good buy.

And guess what: Tony's hunch was right.

Since then, the City lemmings have come round to Tony's way of thinking and there have also been a couple of genuine positive announcements: the shares have gone up by more than 25%.

End result: Tony has now made his clients yet more money.

(Tony is also impressed with my website: or rather, the fact that it makes money. He says he wants me to meet a Very Rich Venture Capitalist mate of his: but I'll believe it when it happens.)

On the other hand, some firms haven't got the knack of good Investor Relations at all: they can't be arsed to keep the key City boys informed about anything and their share price suffers accordingly.

And finally, on the other other hand, some firms just don't have that much good news to report in the first place and make rather sad attempts to dress up not very interesting occurrences as earth-shattering events, e.g. by putting out a press release saying, 'YCC Ltd would like to announce that it has rewired its telephone system and as a result is more equipped than ever before to win several lucrative contracts.' This washes with no one and is a bit sad.

Friday, 14 July

Independent Energy has indeed fallen a bit but my bet automatically closed out when it went below £6,000 so I have now walked off with a *real* cash profit on that one bet: of £5,800. Top! My spread betting losses were threatening to engulf me: they were £14,000, they're now less than £8,000. There is, of course, the small matter of the others that are still up and running (one of which − Geo − is looking bloody awful on paper), but they have until the end of the year to sort themselves out, so I'm not worrying.

Wednesday, 19 July

Earlier on this year so many of my neighbours were babbling on about stocks and shares it seemed like the place had turned into a mini City of London. People I knew only vaguely were stopping me in the road and giving me stock tips. But now the crash has been and − hopefully − gone, things are a lot quieter.

It hasn't stopped people cyberdreaming, though. Everyone, it seems, has a website in, or heading for, cyberspace. Whenever I see Sally she goes on about 'howtospendyourmillion.com', her idea for a luxury goods website, to go along with 'howtomake yourmillion.com', the one we've already got. The trouble is the success of the former depends almost wholly on the success of the latter and, at present, while my portfolio is, as usual, looking healthy and hovering over £60,000, it isn't yet remotely close to fulfilling the first part of the title of this book.

Then there's Mr Bailey, a barrister, who lives opposite. He is Old, and appropriately called Bailey. He took me to Numero Uno's the other day to ask me whether I thought his plans for a legal services website were any good. He intends to offer anyone who's been done for a driving offence a cheap method of dealing with the thing.

And not forgetting Bob the Butcher, purveyor of quality meats to the posh housewives of SW11. He too is planning to conquer the cyberworld, with his vacuum-packed pork loins . . . just as soon as he can get someone to design the website for him.

Going beyond my road, however, there is a fascinating (well, I think so anyway) struggle going on out there in cyberspace. It is nothing less than a battle for the soul of the cyber high street. It is between established, well-known names, like WH Smith and Tesco, and brand-new Net ventures like Amazon.

The WH Smith brigade have two crucial advantages: we, the shopping public, a) know them and b) trust them. Their brand names are ingrained on the public's consciousness.

The new lot need those two things badly: so they're trying to buy them, by advertising. The trouble is, adverts cost millions; and in the end, they may not work anyway.

Another problem is that once the old-guard firms cotton on, good and proper, to the potential of the Internet, the new whizz kids might not be able to compete — no matter how well they've done. Let's face it: if WH Smith really get their cyberact together and start challenging Amazon, who will win in the end? The company with huge profits, a well-known brand name, and loads of high-street shops? Or the newcomer, which exists only in cyberspace, and has debts of millions?

The Amazons of this world might be faster moving, more flexible, and have systems perfectly suited to the Net: but they won't have that advantage for ever.

For what it's worth, I reckon the cyber high street of the future will look not unlike the physical high street of the present — there will be a lot of familiar names, who've learned how to exploit the Net ('bricks and clicks' outfits), alongside a few Internet-only (or 'pure play') niche operators, selling things like exotic plants, or sex aids.

Interestingly, some new Internet outfits are apparently contemplating the one thing they thought they could do without: shops.

Yup, real high-street shops made of bricks, not clicks.

These, the argument goes, would help them win the trust and recognition they so badly need.

God, I've just read this entry back and I still think it's fascinating. Am I boring?

Anyway: tomorrow there is an interesting TV Event If You Like That Kind Of Thing And I Must Admit I Do, Activity: the ITV summer party. Everyone who appears on ITV gets invited to Kensington Palace for an almighty piss-up. There's always something to tell my not – very – impressed friends about afterwards: last year I ended up getting into a minibus with John Leslie of *Blue Peter* and *Wheel of Fortune* fame, and a bevy of women. Leslie went round snogging every single one of them in turn while I held my head in my hands, trying to stop myself from being violently sick. When we got to wherever it was we were going I managed to crawl into a taxi and went home, where I was violently sick.

This time I will try and pace myself.

Thursday, 20 July

23.30: I haven't paced myself that well: it's impossible when blokes with champagne bottles lie in wait all the time, replenishing your glass every time you take a sip.

But at least I'm not as hammered as I was last year. John Leslie was one of the first people I saw: he started laughing as soon as he clapped eyes on me.

'Are ya feeling all right, mate?'

Thankfully he didn't go on for too long about what a pitiful mess I was in last time: he was more interested in stocks and shares and the Net. He said he'd been reading about it in the papers.

It's been a good night out: the problem, as always, was the very start, the bit when I actually arrived.

When you walk into an event like this you feel you know everyone but in fact you know no one: it's just that you've seen them on the telly. So where do you stand? (I mean actually physically stand?) Who do you talk to? I did the Walking To The Bog

Trick a couple of times, then the Pretending To Definitely Look For Someone When I'm Actually Not gambit. Then, thank God, I saw someone I knew, a PR person from ITV, who just happened to be talking to Ramon Tikaram, the bloke who played Ferdy, the bisexual motorcycle courier, in the BBC2 show *This Life*. You know: the dark geezer with the long black hair tied in a ponytail.

He was dead down to earth and we had just got to the possibility of him singing with Surf'n'Turf (his sister, Tanita, had a number one with 'Good Tradition') when the conversation ended abruptly, owing to the arrival of his two co-stars from *This Life*, Daniela Nardini and the one who played Egg's Girlfriend, You Know, The One Who Shagged Her Boss.

Everywhere I looked, there were people who were there, in my front room, while I was growing up.

Oh, look . . . there's Des Lynam chatting to a tasty blonde.

Blimey, isn't that Des O'Connor?

Christ, Dennis Norden is old, isn't he?

And why is Dale Winton a) sweating, b) wearing what appears to be fake tan and c) not listening to a word I say?

Mind you, this year's bash was different: last year, virtually no one I spoke to had a clue who I was, i.e. I fulfilled the definition of a typical D-list celeb: so obscure that only E-list celebs (the lowest ranking of all . . . regional news presenters, etc.) had a clue what I did.

This year, thanks to this project, quite a few people, like Dermot Murnaghan, the ITV newscaster, and Top TV sleuth Roger Cook, started chatting away merrily about stocks and shares. Evidence that a) I am a sad name-dropping twat desperately trying – but failing – to impress you, the reader, and b) that I may well indeed have graduated to the heady heights of C-list celebrity status.

Woof! Truly my life has been changed by this thing!

Sunday, 6 August

23.40: Am listening to the ex-Radio 1 DJ Gary Davies (he ain't no Jeremy Paxman) on Virgin Radio (Radio 2 music for people who can't come to terms with being regular Radio 2 listeners), having played cricket this afternoon, and scored a stupendous 18 runs, and having just seen *High Fidelity*, the (surprisingly good, far better than the book) film of the novel.

I am getting ready to go on holiday for two weeks: a golf tour in Ireland followed by a cricket tour in Devon.

Four thoughts/questions occur to me at this stage of the project – i.e. two-thirds of the way through.

1) It really is deeply worrying that my mood is now being genuinely affected by what happens in the stock market. I am, sadly, happy when I am making money, and sad when I am losing it. The thing is, I never cared that much about money before: this was supposed to be an experiment of the lab kind, where I felt nothing. How can I stop this? Is it normal?

2) The entire world is looking for the killer website idea ... the one that will get everyone logging on regularly, and paying out significant sums of money each time they do. Well, I've got it. The two most popular kinds of site on the World Wide Web are a) porn ones and b) gambling ones: so why not set up a combined porn/gambling site, where people can bet on the events being depicted? Spread betting on how long some of the acts being shown will last. Think about it: www.sexbet.com.

(Hey! Guess what. No kid! I am writing this on my computer and I accidentally clicked on the above website address and ... the frigging thing exists! Try it for yourself! The website has a picture of a naked woman on the front, wearing only a Stetson, and it says things like 'click here for adult-oriented poker'. Didn't someone once say that the only trouble with

great ideas is that someone else has always had them first?)
3) Why are my shares still hovering in the £55k–£65k range,
as they have been for the last three months (see graph table
below)?

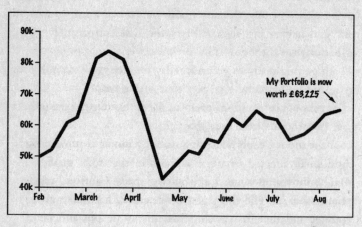

My Portfolio is now worth £63,225

NAME OF CO.	INITIAL STAKE	SHARE PRICE THEN	SHARE PRICE NOW	WHAT'S MY STAKE WORTH NOW, THEN?
Autonomy 1	£30,000	£58.55	£104.50	£30,600*
Autonomy 2	£15,000	£102	£104.50	£15,300
Kewill	£10,000	£19.75	£8.80	£4,400
Oxygen	£2,500	25p	5p	£500
Birchin	£2,500	12p	2.5p	£475
Airtel	£2,500	38p	27p	£1,730
Pace	£2,500	£11.09	8.24p	£1,820
PayForView	£3,500	30p	20p	£2,370
Vocalis	£2,500	£2.33	£2.20	£2,110
Infobank	£4,500	£9.05	£8.25	£3,920
TOTAL				£63,225

* Inc Magic Thursday Profit Taking

As you can see, there's been another burst of activity: I sold my Nike shares for a hefty profit. At last! A successful, textbook bit of investing. In at £18, out at just under £30. Net profit: nearly £2,000. I have blown the lot (the original stake, plus the profit, i.e. £4,500) on . . .

Infobank.

Hi-tech, natch. They were £40 during the Silly Season: now they're £9. But they're not a bunch of spotty graduates with a business plan and no experience: they're a proper company, with proper customers. They specialise in handling commercial transactions over the Net, i.e. they are well positioned to make money. Even if they are making a loss at the moment. And, finally:

4) The most important one of the lot. Sally. Gloriously, her relationship has ended. The Stiff was getting a bit lukewarm anyway, and then last week apparently came out and said, 'Sally, I have to tell you something. There's something missing from my heart.' To which Sally, true to form, replied, 'Yeah. A knife.'

Hmmmm. Plenty to think about over the next fortnight.

Sunday, 20 August

22.00: Just got back from the cricket in Devon and the golf in Ireland. Sally kept text-messaging me, which got me thinking:

1) She likes me, obviously. A lot. But is it time to try and park my tank on her lawn again?

2) I must find out which company makes money from text messaging coz they must be coining it: everyone's doing it! Supposedly, WAP phones – new-fangled mobile things which link you up to the Internet – were going to be all the rage. But who needs to use their mobile to log on to the Net to send a message (slow, tortuous, expensive) when you can text someone (quick, easy, cheap) instead?

As always, the tours were hugely successful off the pitch but not quite as sparkling on it. I scored 3, 0 and 0 in our three cricket games (in the last two I was out first ball) and I didn't manage to shoot less than 100 at golf. However, in mitigation I can plead that I had other things on my mind: halfway through the tour Tony Craze, ex-boxer-turned-stockbroker ('bit warm, bit toppy'), left a message saying that some venture capitalists — real live ones with millions of pounds to invest in new companies — were 'very interested in meeting me', i.e. with a view to, possibly, buying a chunk of the site for a lot of wonga. Which is quite a big deal really.

Oh yes . . . my shares. Not much happening. More excitingly/worryingly, vis-à-vis my spread betting, I'm still £15,000 down. And looking at losses — on paper — of another £20,000. Every cloud has a silver lining, though: at one stage I was looking at paper losses of £30,000. And yes, I've always been someone who thought the glass was half full rather than half empty.

Monday, 21 August
23.45: Feel a bit deflated. Well, quasi-suicidal actually. I gingerly mentioned to Sally tonight, after dinner (another of her medieval banquet jobs), that 'maybe we should kind of explore the possibility, now that we're so close, of getting a bit closer. I mean, people who are going out with each other aren't as close as we are and, like you say, you've got to be in it to win it, so why don't we give it a go, you know . . .'

She did the same thing she did a few months ago: head in hands, sigh, smile. 'Jahnathan, I rilly care for you but there is just soooo much about yew that would drive me crazy.'

'Like what?'

'OK, you rilly want me to tell yew?'

'Go on, then.'

'Yew don't take care of your appearance. I mean, you're so untidy! And you have your weirdo bachelor habits.'

'Like what?'

'Like, you eat at odd times, you chew your nails, you do what you wanna do, when you wanna do it, and you have mango chutney with *absolutely* everything. And you're not exactly in great shape either.'

Blimey. She thinks I'm a fat bachelor weirdo.

Not a lot I can do about that. But the mango chutney accusation seemed a bit unreasonable.

'What's so wrong with having mango chutney with everything? How can the fact that someone has mango chutney with everything be a reason for not going out with them?'

At that point I thought I sounded a little desperate so I left, making sure not to show her how rejected I felt. Again.

Tomorrow we will have to go through the charade (again) of pretending the conversation never happened as we are meeting Tony Craze ('bit warm, bit toppy') to discuss the forthcoming meeting with The Big Cheese Venture Capitalists.

We are having 'talks about talks', as they say in the Middle East.

PART THREE

Striking Oil?

Tuesday, 22 August

17.00: An interesting day. A very interesting day.

Sally and I got a taxi up to Tony Craze's office in the City – he works for a small stockbroking firm called Christows – first thing this morning. She looked distressingly sexy: showing a lot, but not too much, tanned flesh.

The big issue, I said to her, was this: how much of the website do we offer to sell to the venture capitalists, and for how much? We needed to get our story straight before we met Tony Craze, I said, as it wouldn't look too good if we started disagreeing in front of him.

I reckoned we should sell 10% of the site: she had no problem with that. But when I said I reckoned the whole site was worth £250,000 – I don't know why, I just plucked a figure out of the air – she had more trouble.

'Jesus, £250,000 is nothing, Jahnathan. Like that guy earlier this year was offering to sell it for you for five million, for God's sakes.'

'OK, £500,000.'

'£500,000? That's peanuts. Why don't you just go in there and give it away for free?'

'Well, we could say a million . . . just seems like a lot.'

'Jahnathan, they won't even take you seriously if you fuck about. A million is peanuts to these guys.'

I thought about it. She was right.

The big problem is, and always has been, valuing website businesses. There are websites that have never made a profit, and never will, which have been valued at more than £100 million. So putting a notional value of a million on ours suddenly didn't seem so unreasonable.

Blimey. So this is the way things work in the new economy.

When we got into the cab the business was worth £250,000. By the time we'd got to Elephant and Castle it was worth four times that: simply because we'd said so.

Our tactic, then, was to be this: tell Tony that we wanted to flog 10% of the website to his venture capitalist friends for £100,000, and wait for his reaction. The more I thought about it, the more the new valuation made sense: if we got what we were after – i.e. £100,000 for 10% – then that would mean the website as a whole would be worth a million. That would mean that in the space of a few months I would have gone from being a complete e-dunce to a mini Net guru, running a company valued at a million pounds. Which would mean that the title of this book would, in a way, have come true . . . sort of. Which would make an incredible story for the papers. Which would mean lots more free publicity, and the appearance of incredible success. Which would mean lots more traffic to the website. Which would make the thing even more valuable.

Yup. A million-pound valuation was indeed a good idea: a nice round number. Oh yeah: Sally wanted to discuss the possibility of getting the venture capitalists to back her idea for a sister website, too: 'How To Spend Your Million'.

When we got to Christows we were put in a small boardroom-cum-office adjoining the company trading room. A few minutes later Tony Craze walked in and we were off.

I told him about our valuation and he didn't bat an eyelid.

'Jonathan, I don't think that's unreasonable at all, quite frankly; you've got a very valuable little property there and I think the boys I'm going to introduce you to are going to be very interested. And if they're not, I know plenty of other people who will be.'

At this stage a thought raced through my mind: why is he being so helpful? What's in it for him? Will he want paying? Unusually, for me, I kept my mouth shut. He was still talking.

'What I'm going to do, Jonathan, is to tell these boys I'm gonna introduce you to, either to piss on the pot or get off: if they don't make their minds up fairly sharpish, and someone else gets in before them, then they'll have to pay a hell of a lot more for the next ten per cent of the company.'

Blimey. So this is the way it works.

Sally hadn't said anything till that point but then weighed in with her 'How To Spend Your Million' idea.

Tony seemed impressed: and not just with her idea. His whole body language and manner were subtly but noticeably different this time: it was clearly down to the presence of a strikingly attractive, forceful woman. I knew how he felt.

We agreed that he and I, but not Sally, would meet his venture capitalist chums this Friday.

Sally not being there, we all agreed, would be an advantage: if they made me an offer there and then, I could legitimately defer a decision by saying I had to consult my business partner first.

As we left, a familiar figure arrived: 'Mad' Frankie Fraser, the convicted thug and henchman of the Kray twins. Someone in the office who knew him had persuaded him to come in and sign a dozen copies of his new book.

Bit of a coincidence, really: I interviewed him last month, for a piece on *Tonight*. During the chat he described to me, in a completely deadpan East End accent, how he used to chop his victims' legs off with a machete.

And here he was, looking like a lovable uncle, being fussed about and treated like a bit of a hero: in fact he was so sweet and polite to me that I even found myself warming to him a little. As John Lennon once sang: 'Strange days indeed. Most peculiar, Momma.'

Wednesday, 23 August

I am very excited indeed about Friday. I could be a millionaire by the end of this week! Sort of.

Thursday, 24 August

Earlier this year, when Internet madness reigned, the received wisdom (for a lot of people) was that the Net was an easy passport to untold wealth. We now know that to be bollocks, of course.

But what I have found in the last few months is that, with the right idea, it can be a licence to print small, pleasant sums of money: the proof, m'lud, being the cheque for £63.20 which arrived in the post this morning.

Let me explain: someone told me about a company (called Valueclick) which beams adverts down from its HQ on to your website. All you do is log on to their website, fill out a form and, hey presto, a few days later your site gets covered in as many (or as few) on-line ads as you want. The groovy part is this: every time someone clicks you get 14p. So, in the last month, I have worked out, 450 people have clicked on the ads on my site.

I know what you're thinking: why not spend all day clicking, and sooner or later you'll have made enough 14p's to have bought a Saab convertible. Sorry: the techies who run the whole thing have thought of that. They have a system which detects, and ignores, multiple clicking. Sadly.

Another way of coining it is by compiling a list of everyone who visits your site: this can be done by intercepting each one of them, the moment they log on to your site, with a message saying something along the lines of 'Hello, please give me your e-mail address now if you want to carry on logging on to my site. If you won't, then you can't come in. I may give it to interested parties – i.e. banks, share dealing companies, and so on – but I hope you don't mind.'

Once you've got a list of, say, 5,000 of those e-mail addresses, you can sell them – for up to £1,000 a time. Excitingly, the company that buys the list can only use it a certain number of times (usually around 12). After that, if they want to use it again, they have to pay another £1,000.

I, however, have decided not to do this: I don't want to run the risk of pissing my audience off. A lot of them might refuse, knowing that if they gave me their e-mail addresses they would end up getting loads of junk e-mails ('spam') for the rest of their lives. In which case my site would have less visitors and therefore be less attractive for potential investors. I'm probably being a crap businessman, but I don't care: it's my ball (well, Sally's too) and I can do what I frigging like with it.

While we're on the subject of being a crap businessman, Sally has been warning me not to walk into the room tomorrow, when I meet the venture capitalists, with my trousers round my ankles (in the negotiating sense). She has cottoned on, quite correctly, to the fact that I am the world's worst negotiator. As my mate Timo (inventor of Beard Theory) said the other day, when she told him how I'd gone round offering people percentages of the site without them even asking, 'He might as well walk into the room naked, bend over the table, hand them a pot of Vaseline and say "I've bought a full range of cucumbers, sir, go right ahead."'

Friday, 25 August

Today I saw the venture capitalists. There were two of them.

One was called John (tall, big, early forties, brown hair, rugby player type with Manchester accent). The other was called Kevin (smaller, early thirties, blond hair). They have, Tony Craze told me beforehand, £50 million smackers to invest. We met at Christows and Tony (TC) sat in.

I wasn't nervous. Why should I be? I had nothing to lose. Just hyper. I couldn't wait to tell them the story. I began by saying I didn't have a business plan, just 'a very valuable property which I'd like to exploit'. And off I went.

I told them about this book, and how Sally had suggested the website. Then I told them I realised the site would get nowhere unless it got publicity. I knew, I said, I couldn't afford to pay the millions that all those other dotcom companies were spending, and anyway, most of it was crap and ineffective and thus a complete waste of money. So, I said, I got my own. For free. This was the key moment: I took out of my folder every single newspaper article about the site. Not photocopies . . . the originals. They smiled.

'But,' I said, 'did it work? Well, yes it did. Here is the data for the site . . .' At this point I showed them, with a bit of a flourish, the stats: 80,000 hits a week, on average, for the last five months. 'Now I want to capitalise on its success so I'm just talking to a few people to see if they're interested.'

Then TC put his threepence worth in. He didn't actually say these exact words but the gist was pretty much what he'd told me earlier in the week, i.e. 'If you want a piece of the action, guys, you'd better be quick about it as, if you don't want the first ten per cent, someone else will, in which case the next slice will cost you more'.

Somewhere in there he slipped in the £100,000 figure that we're after: he was so smooth about it I almost didn't notice. Their eyelids didn't so much as flicker. Mind you, when you've got £50 million to invest, 100k isn't exactly a lot.

I told them that we had two ideas for the site: one was Sally's idea (i.e. a luxury goods website called howtospendyourmillion.com). The other, I said, was to turn it into a gambling website. 'Because, as you know, the two biggest money-spinners on the web are gambling and porn.'

At this point I thought a bit of bonding might be in order, so I told them my story about www.sexbet.com – which went down well – and TC weighed in with a tale about how someone had asked him to invest in a porn site business. 'The figures were really unbelievable,' he said. (He was referring to the financials, not the physicals.) 'But I just couldn't do it on ethical grounds. I mean, I can't get caught up in all that stuff.'

The tall venture capitalist smiled. The whole thing was very impressive, he said. Blimey, I thought, he's going to write out a cheque right now.

Alas, he didn't.

He didn't think a luxury goods website would work: he'd heard proposals for them before and the problem was defining what a luxury good was. One man's 'luxury good' is another man's necessity and all that. But he liked what he'd heard, he said: he and his mate would go away and think about it. His mate, the smaller one, asked why I didn't turn the site into a financial information portal. Because there were so many of them around, I said: the last thing the world needed was another one. And the ones that were around weren't exactly coining it; one had seen its share price fall by 90% this year, I said.

He nodded. That made me feel good. He'd come up with an idea, I'd pooh-poohed it, and he – a real, live, rich venture capitalist – had deferred to me. They obviously think I know what I'm talking about, I thought. And they respect my opinions. I am talking their language when eight months ago I wouldn't even have been able to hold a conversation with them!

The smaller one asked exactly what kind of gambling website I had in mind. A spread betting one, I said. I could change the site into a spread betting haven: explain to people the attractions (and the dangers) and then, if they opened an account with a spread betting company, I would get a share of the revenues. 'Business to business,' I said. 'Not business to consumer.'

'Will you have one spread betting company on your site, or several?' he asked.

'I dunno,' I said. 'But I quite fancy just one. If you were a spread betting company you'd kill to have the kind of audience I have . . . and the kind of relationship with them that I have.'

He disagreed: he said that if I had all the big betting companies in the UK on my site (there are four) I would be seen as 'an honest gatekeeper'. If I had just one, I'd be seen as their mouthpiece and so lack integrity.

I knew he was right the moment he said it.

We carried on talking for a bit after that: they had another meeting to go to with TC.

As he showed me to the lift, TC patted me on the back. 'That's a killer presentation, Jonathan. I really think you've got them.'

Christ. I hope he's right. We shall see.

Thursday, 31 August

11.43: TC has just left a message telling me to get in touch. This is it!

12.32: No it isn't. The guys want to see something on paper, he said.

Seems fair enough: why should they sign a big fat cheque on the basis of a few verbals? I am going to have to write a business plan.

Trouble is, I don't know how to.

However, I have just rung my mate Gazza, the wicket-keeper in our cricket team, who looks a bit like George Michael after a few burgers, and who does know how to. He says he will give me a hand this Saturday, during our cricket game.

Friday, 1 September

08.00: Fuck. The market is going bonkers. Everything with a hi-tech feel to it is going through the roof. This is just as well: three days ago my spread betting company had £20,000 of my money and on paper I owed them a further £10,000.

Some quick sums. Blimey! If I close all my bets now, I will wipe out the entire £20,000 loss and walk off with a £12,000 profit. A real one!

I am going to hold on, though.

09.34: No I'm not. I'm closing the lot, now, and I'm going to enjoy my weekend.

09.35: Done! I have chased my losses (always dangerous) and recouped them (rare) and made a healthy profit to boot (even rarer). This is mainly due to Autonomy: it's suddenly taken off again. I had four bets in place but the one on Autonomy has made me £26,000 on its own. God, I feel good. And my conventional portfolio investments are back in £80,000 territory too. Woof!

18.20: Just got back from playing golf with Sally. For once my timing (investment, not golf) appears to have been perfect.

The huge surge in share prices this morning was followed by a fall this afternoon. I picked just the right moment to take my cash and run. I was going to sit back and let my profits carry on rising, but the markets are so volatile – hi-tech ones in particular – that you can be sitting on a big fat (notional) profit one moment and then, before you know it, a horrendous loss the next.

As Stevie Winwood once sang (sort of): 'While you see your profit, take it.' (Curiously, this is Sally's favourite song.)

Anyway, I feel a lot better than I have done for some time, and this is why:

NAME OF CO.	INITIAL STAKE	SHARE PRICE THEN	SHARE PRICE NOW	WHAT'S MY STAKE WORTH NOW, THEN?
Autonomy 1	£30,000	£58.55	£117.20	£38,500
Autonomy 2	£15,000	£102.00	£117.20	£19,250
Kewill	£10,000	£19.75	£10.80	£5,400
Oxygen	£2,500	25p	5p	£500
Birchin	£2,500	12p	4p	£760
Airtel	£2,500	38p	25p	£1,600
Pace	£2,500	£11.09	£7.70	£1,700
PayForView	£3,600	30p	20p	£2,400
Vocalis	£2,500	£2.33	£3.42	£3,280
Infobank	£4,500	£9.05	£10.60	£4,980
TOTAL				£78,370

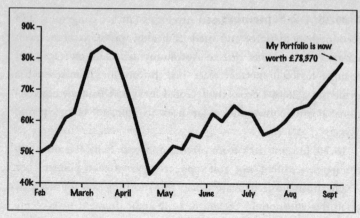

What the above table doesn't show is that I have benefited in quite a big way from unexpected economic developments: when I bought my Autonomy shares, the price was quoted in dollars. (They still are: I've converted them to pounds for this book's purposes.) Back then, £1 was worth $1.60: now it's $1.40. This means that since the pound has fallen by about 12% against the dollar, the value of my Autonomy shares has risen by a corresponding amount.

Nice! Meanwhile . . .

Estate agent (with briefcase) coming round to value house as I am thinking of buying much posher one (with recording studio for 'Surf 'n' Turf', and personal multi gym and mini golf course in back garden) as I may soon be the owner of a company worth one million pounds

"HMMM... needs refurbishing"

Saturday, 2 September

Wrote bizzo plan today, on the boundary, with Gazza's help.

Gazza knows what he is talking about: he has his own Internet company which recently got a big injection of funds from a venture capitalist (VC). This is no mean feat: OK, at the start of the year you only had to say the words 'Internet Start-Up' and complete strangers would be pressing cheques for millions of pounds into your hands. But if you walk up to a VC nowadays and say the same thing you tend to go down like a leper chez Howard Hughes.

So: Gazza has done good.

We both had plenty of time to get on with it: inexplicably, I was out first ball (again) for nought (again). And so was he.

Every so often the ball would come skimming to the boundary, interrupting our little Internet business meeting. Very symbolic: Old Britain meets New Britain.

Anyway, Gazza, making a much bigger contribution off the pitch than he had on it, said two important things: 1) The idea was so good I shouldn't be going to venture capitalists for the money, I should be looking for a loan from the bank. That way, he said, I will avoid giving away valuable chunks of my company which may well turn out to be even more valuable in the future.

He might be right, but if I get the money from VCs, then the site will officially be 'worth' one million quid, which will make the story even better, which will mean even more publicity for the site, which will mean even more traffic.

2) It's all very well asking for 100k, Gazza said, but what are you going to do with it? VCs want to see (look out, jargon coming!) 'their money working hard for them'. If it's nestling in your bank account, it isn't even doing some gentle pedalling on an exercise bike.

Blimey. I hadn't thought of that. Two minutes later, though, I realised there'd be plenty to spend it on. I mean, the website has to be redesigned (the frigging thing keeps crashing): that will cost a few grand. We'll need offices and, crucially, staff. Christ. This is getting serious.

Then we got on to the real meat, and the hardest part of all: predicting what profits I'm going to make in the future. VCs like to see several noughts flying around; trouble is, it's a complete guessing game. I've gone for a profit of £250,000 by year four: I could be wildly underselling myself, but then again I could have overestimated by approx. £250,000. Gazza told me about a bloke who gave some VCs a bizzo plan and they said, 'Hmm. You're only expecting profits of two million by year three. That's not good enough. We're not giving you the money.' So off they went, multiplied everything by five, and came back again: they got the dosh.

I've worked out my all-important profit levels like this:

Every time a customer opens an account with a spread betting company through my site, and spends money, I'll get a cut of the revenues. Normally it's around 5%. Your average spread betting punter places bets worth, on average, £2,000 a year. So for each punter I attract, I'll get 5% of £2,000: £100. In four years, I reckon I can get 3,000 punters using my site (not impossible: only 50,000 people hold spread betting accounts now, but the figure is expected to grow at least threefold in the short term).

So, in four years, I will have an annual income of 3,000 (number of punters using my site) × £100 (my cut of each punter's revenues). Which works out at a handy . . . £300,000.

Blimey.

I will now type it all up and give it to Sally, who is going to make it look all nice and colourful.

Monday, 4 September

Dropped off bizzo plan to the tall VC with the Manchester accent at his office. He seemed completely distracted. Maybe he has bigger fish to fry.

Tuesday, 5 September

He certainly has. The VCs have only gone and frigging bought Christows (the stockbroking firm that TC works for) for £40 million.

The VCs' company is called Evestment: it was worth 12p a share on the stock market. Now it's bought Christows its shares have been taken off the market while all the admin is sorted out. When they return they will be worth a hell of a lot more than 12p.

And it was all going on under my nose, without me knowing!

Then again . . . if I had known about it, I would have been in receipt of some very tasty insider information indeed.

So perhaps it's just as well I didn't.

I wonder if the tall VC would be interested in a small plate of whitebait now he's tucking into a ruddy great Dover sole. I doubt it.

Wednesday, 6 September

You need luck in this game. And I've just had some.

You know last week I was crowing about wiping out all my losses, and walking off with a cheque for £12,000? Well, one of the bets I closed was on Independent Energy. I only made £75 on it: I don't know why I closed it, I just did. I just wanted to wipe my entire slate clean for the time being. Anyway, this week Independent Energy called in the receivers; their bankers won't support their debt levels any more. If I'd stayed in, I'd have lost around £20,000 at a stroke.

Phew!

Tuesday, 12 September

Haven't heard anything from the tall VC. Or indeed the small one. Oh well.

I'm not giving up, though. And neither, it seems, is TC: he has lined up another meeting, this time with Three Very Rich People

Indeed: in Dublin. Turns out they invested £35,000 each, a few years ago, in a small company that is now one of the world leaders in Internet security.

They each bought, roughly, a 5% stake. When they sold out, they made around £7 million each.

I presume they're paying for dinner.

Here we go!

Friday, 15 September

By the way, guess what. I'm still spread betting. I should have tucked away my cheque for £12,000 and had a few small fun punts which would have maybe cost me three or four grand at the most if they hadn't worked out, but I didn't. I weighed in with three big ones. And they're not doing very well. At all. On paper I'm £20,000 down.

(The other day someone told me that spread betting was 'the crack cocaine of gambling'. He's right.)

Saturday, 16 September

I don't believe this. Today I played cricket: I survived the first ball. I punched the air and told the opposition how I'd been out first ball in my last two innings and what a triumph it was that it hadn't happened this time. They laughed. I was out next ball.

Anyway, we (TC and I) fly to Dublin on Thursday.

I must say I'm looking forward to it.

So is Sally: she mentioned that thing to me again today about not walking into the room with my trousers down. I was on the verge of looking her in the eye, not wavering, and saying, 'There's only one place I want to walk into with my trousers down, Sally: your bedroom.' But I didn't.

Too chicken, I guess. Wonder what would have happened if I had?

Tuesday, 19 September
Went round to Sally's for dinner. On the table there was a jar of mango chutney. I couldn't not say anything, could I?

'Blimey. That's significant . . . isn't it?'

She said nothing for a moment. She was obviously thinking. 'Yeah. It is.'

I'm always pleased to see mango chutney on the table: but it has never aroused emotions and thought processes in me like it has tonight.

Friday, 22 September
Got back from Dublin this morning. Interesting night.

Me and TC went to dinner at a place called the Unicorn with the two big-cheese VCs, Charles (glasses, accountant, looked like one) and Malcolm (good-looking, friendly, athletic).

I gave them the spiel I gave the VCs the other week.

Two encouraging things: Malcolm asked me when I needed the money by. I said the end of October. (When I told Sally that this morning she called me a goon. I should have given them a shorter deadline, she said.) And Charles said, 'What I like about your idea is that you've identified real revenue streams.' To which I, most satisfyingly, was able to reply, 'Yes, substantially advertising-based revenue models are a bit outdated now.'

I was dead interested to find out what on earth propelled each of them to invest £35,000 in a company that ended up making them around £7 million each in such a short space of time. Malcolm said, 'Well, you just kind of will yourself towards the winners.'

Charles said it was simply that they both knew the Chief Executive of old, and knew that he would work his bollocks off day and night to make the thing fly, so it was worth a punt.

'You don't seem that chuffed at having made all that money,' I said to Charles.

'Well, no. You see, if we'd stayed in and sold at the top of the market, we would have made seventy million.'

Blimey. Different world or what?

Charles started leafing through the business plan. He pointed out that I'd made myself Chief Executive and Sally Joint Chief Executive. This didn't make sense.

'Either you're *both* Joint Chief Execs or you're not: in which case, one should be the Chief Exec and the other Deputy Chief Exec.'

Oh dear, I said. A mistake. Did it matter?

No, he said. We invest in the person, not the plan.

The meal ended. TC paid. Just as we were leaving, a third bloke turned up: Noel. He looked merry. Noel used to work with Malcolm and Charles and made millions out of the same company: but unlike them, he has since decided to pursue a life of luxury for the time being.

'Hello, Jonathan,' he said, without waiting to be introduced. He then picked a spare copy of the business plan off the table, rolled it up, pretended it was a telescope, and pointed it at my face. 'I want to have a closer look at you.'

Him, me and TC went back to our very posh hotel (the Shelbourne: £200 a night!) for a nightcap.

We chatted for 20 minutes.

'Would you be prepared to accept smaller payments? Like ten thousand for one per cent, rather than a hundred thousand for ten per cent.'

Er . . . I think so, I said. Hadn't thought of that.

All I can do now is sit and wait, I guess.

Friday, 29 September

TC has been on holiday all week. No word from Ireland.

I feel like I'm coming close the whole time but not getting the cigar.

Monday, 2 October

Someone has just e-mailed me to tell me that Mike Lynch has shaved off his beard. What the fuck has he done that for?

I'm going to e-mail him and ask him why.

Wednesday, 11 October

What a surprise. The blokes from Dublin have gone all quiet. I reckon the chances of them sending me a cheque for £100,000 are about the same as the Queen rolling a joint in front of the cameras during her Christmas speech.

Can't say I blame them: the climate isn't exactly conducive to cheque book waving at the moment.

Once again, investors are pulling out of technology shares faster than a priest out of a nun. The same goes for venture capitalists: last year they pumped billions into dot com companies to get them up and running: now, those same companies need more money just to stay on their feet. But the VCs are saying 'enough is enough' and refusing to throw – as they see it – good money after bad.

The latest casualty is Boxman, the internet CD retailer, which has just announced it will be liquidated in two weeks unless it gets an emergency cash injection of 20 million quid.

It's the same old story: while Boxman were burning cash at one end, trying to launch in several different countries at once, it was barely trickling in at the other.

The smell of singed wonga is pretty strong round these parts right now as well: on paper, I am now a whopping £43,000 down on spread bets.

No point in closing them now and accepting the losses though: I'm psychologically prepared for the shares to go all the way to zero.

My strategy now is to pray that the markets bounce back by December: they nearly always do, I'm told, as the commission that the boys in the City get is based on the levels that the markets reach at the end of the year: the higher they are, the more they earn.

Apparently (so the theory goes) the big fund managers are standing by with billions of pounds, ready to pour it in the market any day now.

There's a 'but' here though.

A rather big one.

Most inconveniently, violence has flared in a big way in the Middle East between the Israelis and the Palestinians: in fact it's so bad that they're talking on the news about the two sides being 'on the brink of all out war'.

This is extraordinarily bad news, as it could mean a) The end of the world (literally), and b) The end of the world (financially).

a) doesn't need much explaining: but b) might, so here goes:

If there's a war, the flow of oil from the region will dry up. Therefore its price will sky rocket. (In fact it's already beginning to happen: the price of a barrel has risen by around 10% in the last two days). This will create inflation, and massively eat into the profits of firms around the world, thanks to their increased energy bills. If there are two things stockmarkets hate more than anything, it's the prospect of inflation and lower profits. A slump of Wall Street Crash proportions could be on the cards.

Mind you, thinking about it, if a) happens then I guess we won't need to worry too much about b) anyway.

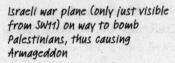

Israeli war plane (only just visible from SW11) on way to bomb Palestinians, thus causing Armageddon

PS: The 'For Sale' sign isn't a joke: I can see it in my front garden, from where I'm sitting. My overdraft is at its limit and I may well need a lot of extra cash: this is the only way to raise it. Richard ('it's peaked') has said I can move in with him if I have to. Blimey. Never thought it would come to this.

Thursday, 12 October
23.00: Spent all day in Leeds, filming. Have been thinking the unthinkable: if there's going to be a crash, should I slam on the brakes and go into reverse, ie

1) close all my bets, take the £43,000 losses on the chin, and then

2) bet everything I have left on the market going into freefall?

If both 1) and 2) happened, I'd make a mint.

But if only 1) occurred, I'd lose everything.

Funnily enough, this evening at Heathrow Airport (I flew back), I spotted Don Cruikshank: the Chairman of the London Stock Exchange no less, who I interviewed earlier this year. I had to talk to him. Omen or what!

We only spoke for two minutes but it was enough to leave me a quivering wreck.

'This is the classic time for an almighty crash,' he said, explaining that October has, historically, always been the worst month of the year for the markets. He reckoned it could – only could, mind you – happen on Monday.

His theory was that traders will have all weekend to get worked up about all the bad news that's around. The Sunday papers will be full of it. On Monday, panic could set in, and . . . goodnight, Charlie.

'But surely it needs a proper declaration of war to happen before everything crashes?' I said.

'Oh no. They only need to *think* there might be a war. Your roll.' He smiled and said goodbye.

Oh God. What am I going to do?

PS: Have just realised what tomorrow's date is.

Friday, 13 October

02.48: 'It's your roll'. That's what the Chairman of the London Stock Exchange said to me a few hours ago. It's been ricocheting through my brain ever since. He's right: I don't know what to do, so I might as well let the dice decide. Or rather the coin. In fact that's what I'm just about to do.

Tails, I will take the £43,000 loss, and bet everything I have left on the market going down. Heads, I will stay put and hope things stay calm.

Tails.

OK. I'll do it first thing tomorrow morning. I have done my

sums and worked out that if the markets fall by 10% or more in the next day/week/month, I will recoup all my losses and make a tasty profit. If they don't fall, it's game over: I will have lost as much as I can bear and I will call it quits. (And move to Norbiton and Richard's back room).

I'm not normally superstitious: but there's something else that strikes me, apart from the significance of today's date. The last big stockmarket crash was also in October. October 1987 in fact. Work it out. It was thirteen years ago. Almost to the day. It's going to be unlucky for someone.

There is some rationality (!) to what I'm doing though: when there are more sellers than buyers, the markets will go down. And not too many people will be buying shares at a time like this. The strong probability, then, is the markets will go down: it's almost certain.

All that matters now are the variables: how much will they go down?

A lot, I hope.

07.59: The market opens in one minute. But I've just spent the last ten talking to Tony Craze (TC). I told him what I was planning to do: and he's talked me out of it. He said he'd spoken to two influential analysts this morning and they all agreed, independently of each other, that there was no need to panic . . . yet. Mind you, he also said I should call him back at 0815. Things might be different then! Oh God. I also rang Mark (my mate in the City who isn't a wanker) and he took the same line.

Both he and TC argue that, yes, the markets will go down a bit this morning. But that will be a good opportunity for some people to steam in and buy some good shares at cheap prices. Come the end of the year, when the expected rally happens, those brave buyers will be patting themselves on the back. Or will they? That's the thing about markets: you never ever *know* what's going to happen. The thing is, I've made my biggest mistakes this year after listening to people who, even they would admit, aren't exactly experts i.e. fat blokes in shellsuits at the dog track, who told me to get into companies which ended up 90% down two weeks later. Now, at the biggest crisis point in the year, I have decided to pull back from the brink and listen to people who've been at it a lot longer than me. Will I be OK? Ask me in December, mate.

23.00: Thank God TC and Mark talked me back off the window ledge: if I'd done what I was one minute away from doing, it would indeed have been game over: not only did the market not crash . . . it actually went up! Strange things, markets.

Wednesday, 1 November
The love affair is over. I have sold my Autonomy shares. All of them. This week the company listed on the London Stock Exchange: Lynchy and co. have used the opportunity to sell another few million quid's worth of their shares, so I thought now might be a good time to join them. Especially since Lynchy has lost the face fungus. (By the way, he responded to my email asking him why he'd shaved it off, but without actually answering the question. He politely declined my offer of Surf 'n' Turf for the Autonomy Xmas party – they're holding it in Barcelona – and he told me how excited he was that he'd recently got to play the saxophone at Ronnie Scott's Jazz Club: but no explanation as to the absence of chin bush. He suddenly seems to have gone all sensitive regarding matters of face topiary).

Anyway, I owe a lot to Lynchy.

I have netted just over 50 grand, in cash: not bad. A profit of nearly 70%. If it weren't for him I'd have gone belly up months ago. Yes, the company are heading for the FOOTSIE 100 and so should go up from here: but then again a lot of people who bought shares in the last two weeks (the price has gone up 20%) might now want to cash in, so the price could just as easily go down. The $64,000 question is this: where will Autonomy be in two years? Opinion is divided. Some say it could rule the world, and the price will double from here: others say it could disappear. I no longer care: I'm out of here.

I should feel elated: I don't. This whole thing has turned into a bit of a nightmare. I have had to endure more miserable, gut-wrenching days in the last year, because of plummeting share prices, than I have in the rest of my life put together.

I can forget making a million: my only aim now is to get out with my shirt intact. My spread betting losses, on paper, are still humungous: around 25 grand. I'm now gambling on the FOOTSIE 100 going up, substantially, by Xmas, to get me out of jail. It's 6,400 at the moment: I need 6,700. Yesterday I spent 92 minutes, non-stop, looking at a live display of the current FOOTSIE 100 price on my computer. Every few seconds it would change . . . up a few points here, down a few there. I wanted to leave . . . but I couldn't.

Last week, I laughed at a story about some cab driving Cypriot share traders in North London who apparently stand in front of their computer screens every day, cheering on the Bank Of Cyprus share price. 'Come on, Bank of Cyprus!' they scream, urging the share on as if it were a horse coming into the final furlong of the Nicosia Derby.

Now I find myself doing much the same thing: except I'm not excited, I'm scared, tired and disillusioned.

God, I want this year to end.

Needless to say, the VCs haven't come calling: my dreams of selling 10% of my site for 100 grand are over.

The only plus point is that it could have been even worse: if TC and Mark hadn't talked me down off the window ledge last month, it would be game over.

And I'm sick of my friends asking me about Sally, and having to say, resignedly and brave-facedly, 'we're just good friends.'

Life is shit at the moment.

Oh, by the way, for what it's worth, here's my portfolio:

NAME OF CO.	INITIAL STAKE	SHARE PRICE THEN	SHARE PRICE NOW	WHAT'S MY STAKE WORTH NOW, THEN?
Autonomy 1	£30,000	£58.55	£115.60	£33,700 (SOLD!)
Autonomy 2	£15,000	£102	£115.60	£16,850 (SOLD!)
Kewill	£10,000	£19.75	£6.87p	£3,440
Oxygen	£2,500	25p	4p	£365
Birchin	£2,500	12p	2½p	£500
Airtel	£2,500	38p	25p	£1,460
Pace	£2,500	£11.09	£5.55	£1,250
PayForView	£3,500	30p	18p	£1,970
Vocalis	£2,500	£2.33	£2.00	£1,920
Infobank	£4,500	£9.05	£7.85	£3,730
TOTAL				£65,185

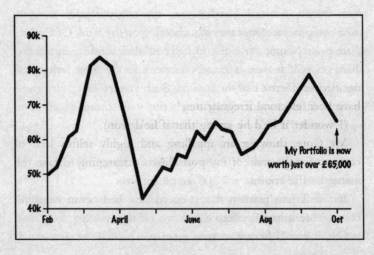

My Portfolio is now worth just over £65,000

Monday, 6 November

I have a problem. It's about Sally. And this book. She's read every-thing I've written so far, except the bits about my feelings for her: I've cunningly edited them out as I'm worried she'll be embarrassed, pissed off, or both.

However, Kate, my editor, and everyone else at Hodder and Stoughton, the publishers of this book, love the stuff about her and they really want me to include it in the final version. But that would mean showing it to Sally. I could just publish and be damned: but I'd feel uncomfortable doing that.

I don't know what to do.

The final version of this book has to be with Hodders by Xmas so at least I've got until then to work out a game plan.

Monday, 13 November

Just when I thought it was safe to go back in the water, back come the crocodiles. In the last two weeks, as the Middle East situation has calmed down, so the markets have gone up: partic-ularly the all-important (for me) FOOTSIE 100. It was even beginning to look as if I might get out with shirt, nerves, sanity and bank balance all healthily intact.

But then came the American Presidential Election Fiasco.

Al Gore, of the (ironically named) Democratic Party, has decided he doesn't like the result: a Bush victory. He claims there have been electoral irregularities.

(I wonder if he'd be saying that if he'd won).

Mr Gore, showing an appalling and highly selfish lack of concern for the state of my portfolio, is threatening to take the matter to the courts.

As we know, markets hate uncertainty. And situations don't come more uncertain than this.

Once again I am in the sickening grip of something over which

I have Absolutely No Control Whatsoever: my spread betting losses, on paper, are now hovering around 50 grand, the level they were at on October 13th (that number again), when I was eyeing up the window ledge. If the much vaunted Xmas stock-market rally doesn't happen – and if Gore carries on acting like a nine year old, I very much doubt it will – then it won't just be the turkey that gets stuffed.

A shard of light amidst the gloom: Sally has invited me round for her annual Thanksgiving beano. I thought it was going to be a big party, but turns out it's an intimate sit down meal: her, me and two other couples. Hmmmmm.

Monday, 20 November

It is time to start tying up loose ends: to find out how all those other DIY traders like Sally Mitchell (Horse Prints Woman), Roger Pritchard (Brotherhood of Man Bloke) and Martin Cockerill (Ex-Gravy Mix Salesman From Leeds) have done. It's also time to interview Martha Lane Fox of Lastminute.com: I've finally managed to set up a meeting at company HQ, just round the corner from Buckingham Palace, later this week. A mate of mine who's met her says she's quite tasty: but looking at her photos, she doesn't do much for me.

Tuesday, 21 November

There is of course one almighty loose end to tie up. Sally. I have decided that I will have to show her this entire book, unedited. She might insist I delete all references to her: she might make me change her name. But following a rare outbreak of ethics on my part (I used to think ethics was a place just outside London where women danced round their handbags) I have come to the conclusion that I really should get her consent before the presses start to roll. You never know: it might even do the trick. And even if it doesn't, I must act with integrity. (Integrity is something

I value very highly: in fact I'm prepared to pay a lot of money for it).

Wednesday, 22 November

Met Martha Lane Fox today. It was all a bit last minute (sorry) as she had been stuck on the tube and turned up 40 minutes late, leaving us only 20 minutes to talk turkey. From a shareholder's point of view, however, this was rather impressive. Martha is clearly not wasting investors' dosh on chauffeurs and limos, she is keeping costs to a minimum.

The first thing that struck me when she walked into the small office was her sexuality. (If you're a *Guardian*-reading, Islington-dwelling, goatee-bearded, cappuccino-quaffing lesbian, and you think I'm being sexist, tough: I cannot tell a lie). She was wearing a tight, black skirt down to her knees, and a slightly less tight, black v-necked jumper which had a fair amount going on inside it.

She sat on the table, cross-legged, opposite me: I was on a chair so my eyes were roughly in line with her fishnet-clad calves. Fishnets! Blimey.

Her photos don't do her justice: she's like a sexy head girl. I didn't fancy her but she certainly had enough sexual presence to put me off my stride a bit.

The first question was easy. The share price. It's a disaster. Lastminute has joined that select (but ever increasing) band of internet companies known as 'The 90% Club': ie, their share price has fallen by roughly that amount since it all went a bit wrong in March. Lastminute were 550p at their height: they recently touched 70p. Was she worried?

'No, I just ignore it,' she said, uncrossing and crossing her legs. 'The important thing is that we have 70 million pounds in cash in the bank and that will see us through to profitability.'

Yeah, but what about all those people who've lost money investing in you?

'The most any private investor could buy was 35 pounds' worth, which isn't a lot of money. Although I have to say the days after the floatation, when the price started falling, were terrible. I got e mails from angry investors calling me "bitch" and "fuckwit" which really upset me.'

I suddenly felt all paternal but tried not to.

What about her press strategy back at the start of the year though: wasn't that a bit of a disaster? Appearing on the front of every magazine and newspaper going contributed to the hype, which in turn fed investor appetite for the shares, which in turn pushed the price up. So when the crash came, there was an awful long way to fall. Looking back, would she have done it differently?

'No. We didn't court publicity, a lot of it found us: you can't stop people writing about you if that's what they want to do. And if you want to establish a brand name, you have to do a certain amount of PR; it's crucial.'

It was time to talk about Martha's barriers to entry. These, you will remember, are one of the things that make companies attractive to investors. The higher the barriers, the more difficult it will be for other companies to get a piece of their action. 'Your barriers,' I said to Martha, 'aren't very high, are they?'

She reddened. Not with embarrassment, but with mild anger, and passion. She leaned forward and started gesticulating. 'No way, no way.'

She started to count them.

'Our brand name, for one: any company trying to do what we do would have to spend tens of millions to get the same level of recognition that we now have. Then there's the cash we've got in the bank, and the five thousand suppliers that we have contracts with. And the 100,000 people who visit our site every day.'

Fair enough, I said: but what about big, established companies like British Airways, who are now starting up their own operations on the Net: they've got most of the above, haven't they?

Yes, she said, but that doesn't mean that Lastminute and BA can't co-exist successfully: the two firms aren't competitors, they're partners: Lastminute sell BA tickets.

Hmmm. I had to give it to her: she certainly believes in the company and is working her (really quite shapely, I couldn't help noticing, as we walked to the lift) arse off to make it a success. She's not in it for a quick buck either: she could have sold some of her shares a few weeks ago and made loads of cash, but she didn't. Not a penny's worth. In fact I feel a bit bad taking the piss out of the company earlier on in this book: Martha, like me, also believed that Something Was Going On Out There and Wanted To Be A Part Of It. And she certainly is now.

Final question: does she get any time to herself or is it work, twenty-four seven?

'God, no. Don't ask me what I did over the weekend. I had a great time.'

'What did you do over the weekend?'

'No, really! I'm not telling you!'

She blushed again: this time with embarrassment.

We shook hands and said goodbye. I liked her. I hope she makes it.

God knows if she will.

Friday, 24 November

00.44: Just got back from Sally's Thanksgiving do. If you are what you eat, then I'm a very large and quite pissed turkey.

Just before I left, I gave Sally the full, unedited manuscript of this book.

'Erm . . . you might find this interesting . . . possibly. Make sure you read it all.'

My powers of prediction vis à vis The Sally Situation are much the same as they are with the markets: I really haven't a clue what's going to happen next. The fact that we were one of three couples round the table this evening could have been highly significant. Then again . . . er . . . it might not.

Oh well, I guess I'll know soon enough. Maybe she's reading it now.

Monday, 27 November

Bumped into Sally on the way back from Mr Samad's the newsagents.

He has achieved the impossible: his shelves, rather like the TECHMARK Index, are at an all time low. How does he manage to survive? (I actually went there not to buy something – which would have been hard – but to photocopy some documents. Surprise, surprise: his photocopying machine had broken down, so I couldn't.)

'Have you read it yet?'

'Gahd no, I haven't had time; I promise I will though.'

I am very tense but bracing myself for the worst.

Friday, 1 December

Oh dear. I braced myself for the worst and it's far worse than I thought: stockmarket-wise, that is. The FOOTSIE, far from rebounding, is plummeting as I write. I am now facing losses of 100 thousand pounds. 100 thousand pounds! And the awful thing is, it could get worse: wise men are now predicting that not only will the FOOTSIE not rally, it will continue to plummet.

Crumbs of comfort? Well, I'm not the only one. TC tells me small stockbroking firms in the City who bought into the Tech dream big time are now looking at losses of a million quid. And on a personal level, those DIY traders I've kept in touch with throughout the year aren't exactly quaffing champagne.

Martin Cockerill, ex-gravy mix salesman, is in a bad way. He is doing this thing full time: he has no other job. He is 20,000 pounds down. He has had to send his wife out to work to make ends meet and spends the whole day, he says, pacing around the house, alternating between frantic despair and depression. He thinks he is going to have to sell his house and buy a smaller one.

'I'm sick of living hand to mouth . . . I'm not suicidal, though. The companies I've invested in, I know they're good ones, I know they'll come back one day. And the wife and me, we've never been happier: now she's out of the house, working, and doing something she enjoys, we're getting on great. If she was here all day, with me moping around all the time, it'd be unbearable.' Clouds and silver linings anyone?

Meanwhile, Sally Mitchell, world famous dog prints woman, has opted for the ostrich-in-the-sand tactic. Last time we spoke, she'd lost the 350 grand profit she'd made, and was back where she started: now she's lost a goodly proportion of her life savings.

'I invested about 100,000 pounds and, quite frankly, I daren't look any more: I'm too scared to see how much I've lost. If I totted it all up, I think I'd get so depressed I couldn't cope.'

She thinks, however, that she may have lost around 75 grand . . . but it could be far more. What effect had it had on her?

'Well, I've always lived a pretty frugal existence . . . which is just as well, because now I haven't got a choice.'

However: Sally, showing the same (blind?) optimism that seems to be sinking so many of us, believes that the good times will return.

'It's got to come back some time,' she said. 'It always does.'

Ahem. This is not necessarily true. Stockmarket history is littered with examples of stocks that have fallen and have never come close to regaining their former peaks: and this year looks like producing a record number of fallen heroes. Talk about learning a lesson the hard way.

Roger Pritchard, Brotherhood of Man stalwart, hasn't suffered quite as badly as the rest of us: only half of his (substantial) portfolio was hi-tech. Even so, his losses may well end up in the six figure category.

'It's going to be the first time in ten years that I make a loss,' he said. 'But you've got to take a long term view; I'm in for the long haul.'

This is one of the many ironies of the crash: investors who got in, hoping to make a quick buck, are now sitting on such huge losses that they have no choice but to sit back and wait for the market to rebound. Which could take years. Then again (see above) it may never happen. This country is now full of Short Term Investors who've suddenly turned into Very Long Term Ones Indeed, overnight.

As for the guys from Katrina and the Waves, I'm worried about them. I've tried to get in touch, but to no avail: I seem to recall Alex, the tall, stringy, posh drummer, talking about investing 100,000 pounds at a time, on the basis that he 'didn't think it was possible to lose that much in one go.'

Eek. If you're reading this, Alex . . . I hope you're OK.

Another thin air merchant is Michael Lusada, the bloke who mortgaged his house to set up EquityTracker.com, the share dealing outfit that took an ad out on my website. I've tried e-mailing him . . . but I ain't heard a sausage. Oh dear. I hope he's all right.

Saturday, 2 December

I've found a winner! From the unlikeliest of sources. Mr Samad, no less: owner of the Worst Little Corner Shop In The Universe.

When I went there this morning for the papers, he and his wife were at a little table at the back of the shop, doling out small paper cups of cheap white wine and small lumps of old cheese at the end of toothpicks. It was a closing down party.

He has sold the shop, and the flat above it, where he lives – for half a million quid !

He says he is going to clear the shelves this evening (that won't take long) and start preparing for a move to Kingston. He is well chuffed: and I'm really pleased for him. There's a moral there somewhere.

Interestingly, his arch rival (and my arch enemy) Mr Bedi has taken to standing outside his shop, arms folded, with a rather smug 'told you so' look on his face. What Mr Bedi doesn't know, however, is that a very posh, very successful supermarket is taking over Mr Samad's premises. The kind of shop, in fact, which will attract Bedi's customers in their droves. He may have won the battle but he's in imminent danger of losing the war: I wouldn't mind seeing his face when the new sign goes up.

Friday, 8 December

Oh dear. It appears I am going to fall short of my target of a million by Xmas. By around a million in fact.

Not to worry: the US election saga looks as if it's drawing to a close, and there has been a small but pleasing bounce in the markets as a result. I am, at least, no longer facing spread betting losses of 100 grand: a victory of sorts, I suppose: but a small and rather sad one – and not the one I was expecting.

This book was supposed to be a 'How to' guide, but I now realise its true value is that it's turned into a 'How Not To' guide. With that in mind, here are my Top Ten Howlers: ie. the biggest and most catastrophic mistakes I've made this year. Take these on board and you will do very well indeed.

1) **I was blindly optimistic**

I've always thought the glass was half full, not half empty; I've always thought England would score twice in injury time and qualify for the next stage of the World Cup, or put on 254 for the last wicket and so win the Ashes. And I've always assumed stocks will go up, not down. This has been a problem. Particularly with my spread bets. My last disastrous foray, at the start of

September, involved me betting on three shares which tumbled inexorably from that moment on. I'm not alone in this: the Great British Investor is conditioned to buy, not sell. That's why spread betting companies say 96% of all bets placed are by punters gambling on the price going up, not down. Had I done the latter, not the former, I would be breaking bread with George Soros and Warren Buffet right now.

2) I followed the herd

At the start of this year, a strange phenomenon occurred: investors started growing fleeces and making weird sheep noises. So did I: I'm surprised someone didn't come after me with a jar of mint sauce. We all bought hi-tech shares because — well — everyone else was. Had we been smart, we would have done the opposite, and shunned hi-techs (many of which have fallen by 90%) and bought into good old-fashioned stocks like Tesco (which has nearly doubled). Of course now that everyone else is selling hi-techs, it is — ironically — probably the perfect time to think about piling in.

3) I put all my eggs in one basket

I knew it was risky when I did it and so it has proved: virtually every share I invested in, or betted on, was in the hi-tech sector. I should, of course, have spread the risk, and looked at brewing, mining or property: but I didn't. As a result, I did the financial equivalent of sending a team onto the pitch with no goalie and 11 strikers: I may have gone 3–0 up, early on, but with ten minutes to go, I'm 8–3 down.

4) I clung onto shares that were falling

Sally (still haven't heard anything) was right: 'Waiting for a stock to rebound isn't investment, it's denial.' The key thing to remember here is to use a stop loss. It will save you an enormous amount of heartache, stress, and most importantly, dosh.

5) I believed what I read

I remember reading, in one of the respected broadsheets,

something like: 'Sometimes it's difficult to see what investors are getting excited about. Not so with this company. This price represents the last affordable level at which private investors can scramble aboard. Buy.'

Six months on, that company's share price has halved. Remember: papers get it wrong as often as they get it right.

6) I didn't take a profit

Had I taken my 6 grand profit on my Autonomy spread bet when it was offered to me, I wouldn't have ended up losing 8 grand on it two days later.

Had I sold my INFOBANK shares at 11 quid, having bought them at 9, I wouldn't now be looking at a 70% loss on them. But then again: If 'ifs' and 'ands' were pots and pans, I'd have a very nice kitchen.

7) I jumped in too quick

I took one look at the pool, saw everyone splashing around merrily, ripped off my clothes, dived in . . . and nearly drowned. Had I waited a few months and got a feel for things, I would at least have been able to tell the deep from the shallow end.

8) I didn't do enough research

I took a tip from a fat geezer in a shellsuit at the dog track: that is not research. I invested in a company whose name I liked: that is not research. Tellingly, the company I looked into the most – Autonomy – gave me my biggest win.

9) I exposed myself to far too much risk

You should only invest what you can happily afford to lose: I couldn't happily afford to lose 50 grand, let alone the 150 grand that I could still theoretically lose, spread betting, if the markets crash tomorrow.

10) I was unlucky

Or maybe just stupid.

At the start of this book, I wanted to find out if being obsessed was enough: obsession had served me (reasonably) well in work, music and sport, so would being obsessed with making money on the stockmarket, in itself, be enough to make pots of dough?

The answer is no. In fact it's probably a disadvantage. Being obsessed tends to make you hysterical when you should be calm: in this game you need good judgment, experience, and a cool head.

If I knew then what I know now . . .

Sunday, 10 December

Bumped into Sally on the way to Mr Bedi's. I didn't want to hassle her again about whether or not she'd read the manuscript, so I managed (just) to avoid the subject. Instead we discussed whether or not I had lost the moral high ground by returning to Mr Bedi's as a customer even though a few months ago I vowed to boycott him for ever.

She thinks I've made myself look like a bit of a prat: I think I've made my point.

Anyway: maybe she's read it and is consulting her lawyers. But then again, maybe she hasn't. Have I written the longest emotional suicide note in history? I may be an optimist but I'm pessimistic on this one: if she wanted to start something between us, she would have done it by now, surely?

I can do no more: I have made my final throw of the dice.

Monday, 11 December

The end is nigh! At last! Kate, the editor of this book, has demanded that I deliver the final pages to her by 9am next Monday. And then I will be free. Oh God, how have I longed for that day to arrive!

I have had the odd euphoric day this year, it is true; getting off my exercise bike to find that I was several thousand pounds richer than when I got on it, was definitely one. But the good days have been horribly outnumbered by the bad.

In fact, I have had more panic-stricken, stomach-stewing days of nausea this year than I have in the rest of my life put together. (Actually, come to think of it, I never had any days like that until I started this frigging thing.)

Soon I will be able to watch the news again without feeling the contents of my belly lurch downwards when the headlines announce MIDDLE EAST ON THE BRINK OF ALL OUT WAR.

Soon I will be free from the Pavlovian fear and trembling I feel the moment my mobile phone rings in the middle of a bad day on the markets: 'Sorry to bother you, Mr Maitland, but we need another 20 thousand pounds from you by midday tomorrow if you want to keep your bets open.'

Soon I will be able to sleep properly instead of spending entire nights lying on my back staring at the ceiling, fretting over the fact that yet another manufacturer of semiconductors has announced that their fourth quarter profits are going to be slightly less than expected and knowing that in a few hours the markets will plunge as a result and there's absolutely nothing I can do about it.

And soon, thank God, I will be free from the uniquely distressing and frightening sensation of turning on my computer screen and seeing it covered in little red arrows pointing downwards.

Now I know what it must feel like when you're in a lift and the cable snaps and it suddenly plummets at the rate of 90 floors a second.

Mind you, in a way this has been worse: at least in the lift scenario the fear only lasts a few seconds and then it's all over. I've managed to prolong the agony for nine months.

Soon my emotional and psychological wellbeing will not depend on whether the share price of some obscure software company has a '+' or a '–' next to it.

Oh yes. Soon I will be free.

Friday, 15 December

It is over! Hallelujah! There is good news (two lots, in fact). There is bad news. And there is no news. Let me explain:

1) **The Good News**

Despite my errors, I have done rather well in my conventional investments. I've turned my original 50 grand into just over 62 grand. An increase of nearly 25% in a year. Most investment firms judge their performance by comparing it to the FOOTSIE 100, which is almost certain to end the year considerably lower than it was twelve months ago: by around 5%.

I have 'outperformed the market', as they say, and positively beaten some City professionals into a cocked hat: The Aberdeen European Technology Fund, for instance, which many private investors poured money into at the start of the year, has fallen by more than 50%. And they're not the only ones. Any stock-broking or investment firm that got heavily into hi-techs, ie. most of them, has been badly burnt.

The TECHMARK, which measures the value of the top hi-tech companies in the UK, has had more than 40 billion quid knocked off its value this year. (Where did it all go? Into the pockets of those who were wise enough to sell in March: ie. the likes of Luke Johnson (Mr Pizza Express) and co.)

The key to my success here was that I gambled big on one share and, crucially, got out at the right time. By turning my Autonomy shares into cash when I did, I safeguarded my original 50 grand . . . the money from my other (appallingly badly performing) investments was the icing. So: here's the final graph, and table.

NAME OF CO.	INITIAL STAKE	SHARE PRICE THEN	SHARE PRICE NOW	WHAT'S MY STAKE WORTH NOW, THEN?
Autonomy 1	£30,000	£58.55	N/A (Sold)	£33,700
Autonomy 2	£15,000	£102	N/A (Sold)	£16,850
Kewill	£10,000	£19.75	£4.62p	£2,310
Oxygen	£2,500	25p	3p	£270
Birchin	£2,500	12p	2p	£380
Airtel	£2,500	38p	23p	£1,470
Pace	£2,500	£11.09	£5.15	£1,140
PayForView	£3,500	30p	22p	£2,420
Vocalis	£2,500	£2.33	£1.62	£1,540
Infobank	£4,500	£9.05	£4.10	£1,950
TOTAL				£62,030

(By the way: since I bought my Autonomy shares, there has been a 3-for-1 share split. That means instead of having, say, 10,000 shares at 90 quid each, an investor suddenly had 30,000 shares at 30 quid each. To keep things simple, I have quoted the pre-share split price throughout this book).

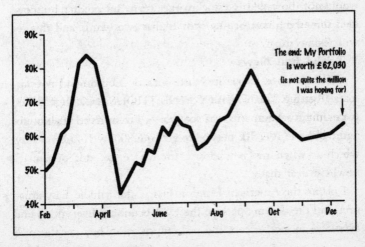

The end: My Portfolio is worth £62,030 (ie not quite the million I was hoping for)

So: what went wrong with my other shares? Er, we've been through that. Irrational exuberance, etc etc. Or, to get more technical for a moment: a completely unsustainable amount of growth was built into hi-tech shares at the start of the year. Some prices assumed growth rates of something like 40%, year after year, for ten years. This non-stop, turbo-charged, explosive growth was never going to happen. It was like saying a sprinter could break the 1500 metres world record simply by running 15 sets of 100 metres flat out without stopping. Not even Microsoft, in its heyday, managed 40% growth, ten years on the trot. So, every time a Hi-Techie said, 'Sorry, we got it wrong: we're going to grow by 35% next year, not 40%', which has happened every week now, for months, the hi-tech market as a whole got slaughtered.

Ironically, 35% growth is exceptional: but it's not turbo-charged. Just reasonably explosive. And for a market which was programmed to expect turbo-charged, 'reasonably explosive' wasn't good enough. So: just as prices got ludicrously high on the way up, they got correspondingly butchered on the way down. They set the bar too high; we all paid the price.

Having said that, if I'd stuck to conventional investment, I would now be hailed as a stockmarket guru. But I didn't. I discovered something that begins with 'S', has two words, and rhymes with 'bedwetting'.

2) The Bad News

OK, here goes. I have lost just south of 39 thousand pounds, spread betting. Yup. THIRTY-NINE THOUSAND POUNDS. It could have been worse: a lot worse. I'm relieved it's not six figures. The FOOTSIE needed to get to 6,800 by 10.00am today, which is when my bets closed, for me to get out of jail: it's nowhere near that.

I blame the American Election Fiasco, the Middle East situation, and the slowing pace of the USA economy. Everything and everyone, in fact, except the real culprit: me. They say the well adjusted gambler regards his losses as the price of his entertainment (ie. you might lose 300 quid on the dogs but at least you've had a fun, sociable time) but I haven't even had that. Losing 39 grand spread betting has been a lot of things, but entertaining? Er, no.

Ironically, I have got quite good at it recently: as part of my research for this book I opened a second betting account last month, with a different firm, with 5 grand. I've just closed it: having doubled my money.

I am never spread betting again. (Well, OK . . . not as much as I have been anyway).

3) The Good News (Part Two)

The reason I am not filing for bankruptcy is that over the year as a whole, I have actually made money. No kid. Thanks to the Internet.

My website project has made me a profit of just over 36 grand: £36, 245.27p, to be exact. In other words, the (roughly) 40 grand I lost spread betting, I have (all but) recouped through the Internet. Factor in the money I've made from conventional investing, and I've ended this year just over 8 grand up, ie. a mere £942,000 short of my target.

OK: I have failed. But at least I had a go. Something Was Happening Out There, And I Was A Part Of It.

About that £36, 245.27p: almost two thirds came from advertising, sponsorship, and commissions (ie. money paid to me by firms whose books/newsletters/training courses etc. were bought via my site.) The rest came from this book, and the articles about the project. You might think it's cheating, including money I made from writing about this: I don't.

This book is called 'How To Make Your Million From the Internet', not 'How To Make Your Million From The Stockmarket'. And making money writing *about* the Internet is a perfectly valid way of making money *from* the Internet: possibly *the* best way, in fact. (Mates say I'm like those people who place ads in the papers saying 'Make a million! Send one pound and I'll tell you how !', and then hope they get one million replies: I see their point, but I like to think this is more sophisticated).

But will this book make me a million? Well, it's had several thousand advance orders before it's even finished, it's being serialized in the national newspapers, and it's been awarded the honour of being named WH Smith Book Of The Month (Travel, Non Fiction Section) for February 2001: which, Kate the Editor tells me, is A Big Deal. (This gives me immense pleasure: I love awards, but have only ever won one: the Epsom College Chess Championship, 1978. Even then, I never actually won the final: the semi finalists in the other half of the draw never got round to playing, so I won by default).

OK: It'll be hard to make a million from this book: to do that, I need to sell just under a million copies. (I get one quid for every book sold). But not impossible: I mean you've bought it, for a start. (Thanks ever so much: I hope you've enjoyed it. By the way, if you want to e-mail me, you can do so via my website: www.howtomakeyourmillion.com. Just click on my name at the bottom of the home page. Bouquets and brickbats equally welcome).

But that's not the point, really. What I've shown, I think, is that Anyone Can Be A Part Of It. 'It' being The Great Internet Revolution. I have created a secondary income, from the Internet, which easily exceeds the average national wage: and if I, a complete cyberdunce, can do it, anyone can.

I know you'll say, 'But you have a privileged position; you're in the Media, not anyone can do what you've done.' Well, with respect, you're wrong. Anyone can, provided they have a good enough idea. Take Bob the Butcher: purveyor of vacuum-packed pork loins to the posh housewives of SW11. He has started a website, to go with his existing business. It is on course to make him an extra 30 grand per annum. This is because he is now getting bigger orders, from more customers. Bob is not in the Media: but he's making the Net work for him, just like I have (thank goodness).

What I've learnt is this: the received wisdom, in cyberspace, was that to make loads of dosh, you had to 'Get Big Fast'. That was Amazon.com's mantra. That meant spending billions and expanding incredibly quickly. Trouble is, as a lot of Net companies have found, if you get too big, too fast, you can end up getting very small, very fast, too.

For the likes of you, me, and Bob the Butcher, the more realistic option is: 'Get small, very slowly.' And then, 'Get slightly bigger, even slower.' You might not make a million overnight: but you may well end up making a nice little packet on the side. And if you stick in there, who knows what might happen?

I am (sticking in there, that is): my site is staying up there in cyberspace and possibly joining forces with another one. The latest news is that TC, my stockbroker pal ('Tipster To The Stars' is how he's introduced on TV these days), is currently persuading his new bosses to pump 250 grand into a new website, which I will help him devise, run and publicise. TC is offering Evestment 20% of it, in return for their money: he says they are very interested. If it happens my stake will be worth 150 grand. Or rather 'worth' 150 grand.

The idea is this: people will log on to www.tonycraze.com and subscribe to a monthly newsletter detailing his hot (and not so hot) share tips. This is actually quite a good idea. Every time TC appears on telly he gets hundreds of e-mails asking him to repeat what he's tipped. Clearly, there are plenty of people out there prepared to pay for his words of wisdom: a lot of financial newsletters like this cost 100 quid a year. OK, I know not all of TC's tips have done great; a few have been absolute dogs: he admits that. But what makes this idea a goer is that it's a lot less risky using his advice as a starting point (given that he's spent every day for the last thirty years looking into these things), than it is using a Ouija Board. Or a fat bloke in a shellsuit at the greyhound track.

Will it happen? Will my stake *really* end up being worth anything, rather than a notional amount? Dunno. Don't really care. I've been here before, of course: with the boys from Ireland, and the bloke who offered to sell my site for 5 million. Nothing came of either. But as Sally says: 'You gotta be in it to win it.' And at least I am officially now A Part Of Whatever It Is That is Going On Out There.

So where does that leave my house?

Spreadbetting missile which was always headed my way and which has now hit its target causing massive damage

The man from the internet insurance company who is going to pay for all the damage, thank goodness (and may yet end up paying for new house with studio, putting green, etc)

4) **No News**

Hmmm. Sally. She rang an hour ago. She is staying in tonight, and reading the manuscript in one go. She promises she will give me a verdict by Monday.

I'm going out. For a massive Xmas drinking/karaoke fest.

Saturday, 16 December

12.05: Sally just came round. Her eyes were a bit moist. She had the manuscript in her hands. She stood there, on the doorstep, looking at me. For about 4 seconds.

I gave her a look that said, 'Well?'

She moved towards me.

You know that delicious sensation when you suddenly realize, with absolute certainty, that something wonderful is going to happen, before it actually does? Like in cricket, when you're shaping up for the perfect cover drive, and you know the ball is going to the boundary, before you've even made contact? Well, this was better. She was going to kiss me.

And then . . . she kissed me. Properly. For quite a long time in fact.

'It's beautiful, Jahnathan, beautiful.'

'You don't mind then?'

'No. No. Not at all. Not at all.'

We kissed again.

Blimey. What a year. I may not have made my million – yet – but I may, just may, have stumbled into something far more valuable.

PART FOUR

Hows and whys; do's and don'ts

(the serious bit)

Where to go for financial information on the Web

Finding a share-related website to suit your tastes is a bit like finding a decent curry house: there are loads to choose from and at first sight they all seem bewilderingly similar. The good news is that, most of the time, financial sites, unlike tandooris, offer their products free of charge.

I suggest you try as many as possible (financial sites, that is). You probably won't find, and certainly shouldn't settle for, a single site to satisfy your needs. Being as well informed and as far ahead of the pack as possible with news on particular companies often makes the difference between winning and losing on shares, so you should experiment and bookmark a few sites that catch your eye, and then regularly review your choices.

On-line newspapers

Useful ports of morning call are the Internet versions of newspapers. On some there is an element of yesterday's news today, but exclusive stories, analysis, editorial comment and tips can move share prices sharply. Tips in the Sunday business sections will be particularly influential on a Monday morning. Beware, though: if it's in the papers it may be too late.

Associated Newspapers' *Evening Standard* and *Daily Mail* are at www.thisismoney.co.uk, the *Guardian* at www.guardian unlimited. co.uk, the *Independent* at www.independent.co.uk, the *Daily Telegraph* at www.telegraph.co.uk, and *The Times* at www.the times.co.uk.

Financial sites

Bloomberg
www.bloomberg.co.uk
The news service and stock market reports are quick and accurate, but it is more a taster of what a Bloomberg terminal can do. Not great for checking prices, but if you do it opens up neat

corporate snapshots, price graphs, financial data and a news section featuring recent Bloomberg stories about the company in question.

Breaking Views
www.breakingviews.co.uk

A recently established site run by a team of experienced financial journalists which concentrates on the main British company news of the day. A crisp, clean site design, with an emphasis on analysis as well as news stories.

Brokerlink
www.brokerlink.co.uk

Provides research reports on about 40, mostly small-cap, British listed companies. It's pot luck as to whether there is a report on any company stock already in your portfolio, but you might get lucky. What info is there is quite good but most of it looks a bit dated. Useful links to about 1,500 UK listed company websites, though.

Citywire
www.citywire.co.uk

Easy-on-the-eye site design with lots of unique news content, written by a team of experienced journalists. It's a clean, simple and effective financial news service, but you'll have to look elsewhere if you want lots of additional features.

CNN
www.cnnfn.com

The financial news service of CNN. Look out for the world news section and then select the European news, which has a heavy British slant. A quick, easy read for anyone looking to get up to speed on the big company and financial news stories of the day. Also has excellent US markets coverage – useful if you want to know how the Dow and NASDAQ performed overnight.

Daytrader
www.daytrader.co.uk
Good-looking site with tips and hints for the novice investor. The site has added some extra content to what was a spartan offering, but it is still thin. Has a decent daily press round-up, though.

DigitalLook.com
www.digitallook.com
An excellent site for novice investors, with a financial directory giving lists of on-line brokers and resources, and lots of easy-to-follow advice. Takes news feeds from a variety of different sources. Free company e-mail alerts service.

Financial Times
www.ft.com
Finding your way around the site can be a bit of a potholing exercise, but it has two excellent features – a searchable news cuttings archive, and Barra's detailed brokers' forecasts of company performance – which help make amends.

Find
www.find.co.uk
Lists 1,500 UK financial websites. Comprehensive and well-ordered reference tool for company news junkies looking for fresh information sources, or relevant websites.

Fucked Company
www.fuckedcompany.com
An American website that follows the misfortunes of the dotcom

world Stateside, but strays into the British rumour mill when it gets a chance. It seems to us that some of the story sources may be disgruntled employees ratting on their own companies, so the content may have to be taken with a pinch of salt.

Hemmington Scott
www.hemscott.com

A top finance website with a smart layout, and bags of excellent background reference data on companies. The free UK Equities Direct section of the site (http://www.hemscott/equities) includes comprehensive statistics on all UK main market and AIM-listed companies, consensus broker forecasts, share price graphs, lists of company advisers, contact numbers, 15-minute-delay stock prices, and lots more. The premium service offers live company news straight from the exchange, a fuller news service, and a results forecasting service by broker.

Interactive Investor International
www.iii.co.uk

Offers free company and economic headlines. Look beyond the heavy personal finance angle and you will find lively bulletin boards, news, prices and commentaries. Handled the on-line applications for the retail portion of the Lastminute.com share offer, and promises that more share offers are on the way.

Investors Chronicle
www.investorschronicle.co.uk

The on-line version of the well-known Friday magazine provides useful directories of stockbrokers and an on-line bookshop, as well as selected stories from back issues of the magazine.

London Stock Exchange
www.stockex.ie/

The home site of the London Stock Exchange. Contains a useful price-checking section, and a walk-through of how the market works.

Market-Eye
www.market-eye.co.uk

Designed to resemble a trading terminal. Datastream/ICV news and statistics, delayed by 15 minutes, are free, and the bulletin boards are lively. The number-crunching tools are excellent, allowing savvy investors to download data such as closing share prices.

MoneyWorld
www.moneyworld.co.uk

Market reports, news and lots of juicy features including graphs, charts and portfolio management tools.

Motley Fool
www.fool.co.uk

There is lots of content here but the style can be pretty quirky. The message boards discussing companies and their shares are well designed and popular, though.

Multex
www.multex.com

The British operation of an American parent. Handy for research and brokers' reports, many of which are free, from an Internet operation part owned by financial news giant Reuters.

Newsnow
www.newsnow.co.uk

Collects news from lots of different media and sources, divided into technology, financial and general news sections, on a well-organised site.

The Register
www.register.co.uk

A slightly nerdy site concentrating on technology, Internet and computer related stories and companies. Sometimes quirky and irritating, but pretty useful if you are into Net and technology gossip.

Reuters
www.reuters.co.uk

The news and financial information giant whose costly news terminals are most favoured by professionals provides delayed and selected news feeds to clients such as Yahoo! and Lycos. Reuters isn't giving much away here other than a few headlines stories and headline numbers for the Dow, FT–SE and Nikkei.

Sharepages
www.sharepages.com

Excellent share price charts, equity trading profiles, statistical analysis, directors' share dealing details, and other impressive content. Unfortunately the layout is a bit of a mess. Sunday newspaper tips summary.

Stocknet
www.stocknet.co.uk

Claims to be the only site in the UK to offer real-time share quotes. The only catch is you have to use themutual.net as your Internet Service Provider. Charts from bigchart, news from AFX news wire and company details from Hemscott.

UK Invest
www.ukinvest.co.uk
UK Invest runs a clean, easy-to-read site with an excellent 15-minute delay share price service. Detailed coverage of losers and gainers, price movements, snappy stock market reports, handy broker recommendation pages, and links to UK regional investment clubs. Comprehensive company data.

Venturedome
www.venturedome.co.uk
A useful site for keeping up to speed on the latest dotcom-related financial news and trends, in a neat, well-designed package. Also contains useful advice for dotcoms looking for new or additional funding.

Yahoo! Finance
http://finance.yahoo.co.uk/
Useful for quotes, general overviews and graphs, also some Reuters news, but it's best as a quick summary of major events.

Trading Shares On-line

Increasingly popular, buying and selling stocks and shares via the Internet accounted for about a fifth of all private share transactions during the hectic hi-tech share boom in the first four months of 2000. That has tailed off a bit now, but on-line trading is a huge growth area and has opened the world's stock markets to private investors as never before.

How It Works

First you will need to register with a stockbroker, which allows you to buy and sell listed shares through the Net. You can normally do this through the broker's website, but for legal reasons there will be some post involved too. On-line dealing is cheap because it is usually execution-only, meaning you make your own decisions about which shares to buy and sell, without advice from the broker.

You will normally need to open an account with your chosen on-line broker, who will fund your share purchases and collect the proceeds of your share sales. Any dividends will normally be paid into the account. If you have cash in the account, you will earn interest on it. If you have to set up an account you might have to wait a couple of weeks for it to be activated before you can trade. You'll be given a personal identification number or a password that will allow you to trade on-line.

To trade shares, simply request the price of the shares you want to sell or buy. Then, if you want to go ahead and trade, you confirm it on-screen and the deal goes ahead. The money to settle the deal is taken from your account, or if preferred charged to your credit or debit card.

Of course, you don't have to trade on-line: many still prefer the good old-fashioned telephone method. Don't worry: no one will laugh at you.

Costs

The cheapest Internet brokers will buy or sell your shares for around a tenner plus stamp duty, and many are doing away with the old way of calculating the charge by taking a small fixed percentage of the total transaction. Remember: if you are going to be trading a lot, say more than a couple of times a week, then dealing charges are going to be an important part of your costs.

But dealing prices change as fast as the fledgling on-line broking industry itself. Lots of new stockbrokers looking for Internet share traders have pressed dealing charges to all-time lows and made it much easier for anyone on the Internet to buy and sell shares.

Choosing the right broker for you can be a bewildering business (it's curry-house time again), and low dealings costs should not be the only concern when picking an on-line broker, so go through the checklist below before you sign up.

If you want to use the phone to trade, be aware of horror stories of investors holding on the line for an hour, while the price of the share they are waiting to sell plummets.

One way of avoiding this is to sign up with two brokers so that you have a greater choice when it comes to service, trading and reliability. In which case don't worry if you can only get through to Broker No. 1 when it's Broker No. 2 who holds your shares: Broker No. 1 will normally sell them for you, for a small charge.

What to Look out for

- First, check that your computer is happy with all areas of a brokers' site, and that it doesn't take an irritating amount of time to download the pages. Some even let you have a practice run at ordering shares. You should feel confident using the site.

- Check that the site has a good track record and high security. If it's a secure site you should see a small closed padlock appear somewhere in your browser window. That means your orders will be encrypted – i.e. the information will be securely protected – and you can have a high degree of confidence that the information you provide, such as account numbers and your home address, will not be picked by some unscrupulous nerd wanting your details to pay for premium Web porn.

- Dealing charges will be a more important consideration for investors who trade a lot. If you only make the odd trade you can probably afford to cast your net a bit wider and look for added extras such as research and reliability.

- Some new market entrants have special introductory offers such as no dealing charges for a month. So if you don't have a broker already, keep the bargain antennae switched on.

- Check exactly what you get for your money. Some companies will have lots of hidden extras such as charging for printed

statements. Others will throw in freebies, such as Internet security, free company research, excellent customer support, accurate billing and accounts, portfolio tracking, quick
order-processing, and even financial news. Check how many
days you will be given to settle transactions, and what happens
to share certificates.

● If you can, check how long it normally takes for the broker
to execute your order. It should be as close to instantaneous
as possible, but on busy days, when there is a large order backlog,
it has been known to take the best part of an hour from the
time you place an order to the actual trade taking place, in
which time prices can change.

Who Does What

Most of the high-street banks offer an on-line share dealing
service, and though that may cut down on the administrative
hassle, they are not necessarily as cheap as specialist Internet
brokers. The list below is by no means comprehensive, so if you
don't like what you find keep searching the Net until you find
a broker that really suits your needs. (NB: The information below
was collected in October 2000. Some of it – e.g. the dealing
charges – may have changed by the time of publication, so make
sure you check.)

Barclays
www.barclays-stockbrokers.com
Charges flat 1% commission per deal, minimum £11.99, maximum
£39.99. Barclays will normally debit the cost of your purchase
from your bank or building society account by direct debit ten
business days from the date of the deal. For urgent trades you can
pay for your first purchase by cheque to allow time for your direct
debit to be set up. The initial dealing limit is £7,500.
  Tel: 0845 6090039.

Charles Schwab
www.schwab-europe.com
There is a minimum £12 fee per trade on deals up to £1,000 and a progressive fee scale depending on order size up to a maximum of £50 for large deals. Money on account attracts interest of between 1% and 4.75%, but the juicy part is that the first 30 days' on-line trading are free.

Tel: 0870 608 0140.

Comdirect
www.comdirect.co.uk
The on-line broker service of Germany's Commerzbank, which has a big British presence and a user-friendly site. Charges are just £5 for deals of less than £500, £12.50 up to £5,000, and £14.50 for bigger deals, as well as a £25 annual fee. The service includes news headlines, an investment club and a deal with Internet 'currency' beenz, which can be exchanged on some other sites for goods and services.

Tel: 0870 600 6044

Cortal
www.e-cortal.com
Seems to be the only site currently available offering its clients access to all the main European stock markets. It also offers New York and NASDAQ among a total of nine tradeable markets, including London. Owned by a major French bank, e-cortal claims to have over 550,000 users. Your account is held in euros, so there are foreign exchange considerations.

Tel: 08000 287081.

Deal4Free

www.deal4free.com

A novel way to trade shares and a genuine alternative to spread betting, Deal4Free trades CFDs, or Contracts for Difference, a kind of option related to share price movements. This is dead complicated and beyond the ken of non-experts, i.e. 99.99% of the people reading this. Mind you, trading is free and gains are untaxed. Ideal for day traders looking to make rapid deals, but not for the inexperienced or occasional trader. Also offers foreign exchange and options trading.

Tel: 01992 535550 or 08000 933633.

Donaldson, Lufkin & Jenrette

www.dljdirect.co.uk

This well-known broker charges a single-level commission rate of 0.75% – with a minimum charge of £14.95 and a maximum of £37.50. No annual account fee.

Tel: 0800 358 4477.

E*Trade UK

www.etrade.co.uk

Charges are based on how often you trade. Its flat fee for deals under £1,500 is £14.95, rising to a £24.95 maximum. After 25 deals all trades are £14.95. Opening account balance is £1,000. There's a £25 bill every six months.

Tel: 08000 525000.

Fastrade

www.fastrade.co.uk

Quick and efficient, it takes a basic 0.5% commission on deals, but charges a minimum £15 per deal and a maximum charge of £30. Dealing in any overseas securities will be charged at 1.8% of the amount with a minimum charge of £30.

Tel: 0131 247 7399.

Halifax ShareXpress Online
www.halifax.co.uk

Doesn't demand a separate account and you can pay for your shares with a debit card. Charges range from £12.50 to £50 depending on the size of the transaction. Go to the halifax.co.uk home page, choose the products and services menu at the top right of the screen, and scroll down to share dealing.

Tel: 0990 336644.

iDealing.com.
www.idealing.com.

It has a flat charge of £10 (plus 0.5% stamp duty) regardless of the size of the deal. However, you do have to open an account with at least £500. Interest is paid at a rate of 5% gross (4% net) and there is a £5 administration charge every three months. Customer services only via e-mail.

Killick and Co.
www.killick.co.uk

Killick and Co. offer a full broker service including research and recommendations but appear to be going for the upper end of the market with punters needing to deposit a minimum £10,000 to trade on-line. The minimum charge is £30. Commission charged at 1.25% with an additional charge per deal of £2.50, plus an annual £10 fee.

Tel: 0207 337 0400.

MyBroker
www.mybroker.co.uk

Charges a flat fee of £25 plus stamp duty and $15.95 on all American share trades. You can trade options too, and it's also promising European share trading soon. Targeting regular investors, the site charge is £10 if you don't trade for a month.

Tel: 020 7903 6350.

NatWest
www.natweststockbrokers.co.uk

Charges 1% on the first £4,000 then 0.1% over that, plus stamp duty. There is a minimum charge of £15 plus an extra £3 per trade if you want certificates rather than holding the shares in a nominee name. Registration is free of charge, but you don't need to open an account. Instead, your bank account is debited or credited when you buy or sell.

Tel: 020 7895 5880.

Nothing Ventured
www.nothing-ventured.com

This is the on-line new issue and share dealing service of Durlacher Limited, a broker specialising in technology companies. There is a fixed £11.50 charge, plus 0.8% commission on the first £2,500, then 0.15% above this up to a maximum £70. The annual fee is £50.

Tel: 0207 459 5700.

Redmayne Bentley
www.redm.co.uk

Minimum charge is £12.95 on transactions up to £2,590. Charges then rise on a 0.5% commission basis to a maximum £39.95. Good, uncluttered site design. Real live prices prior to trade execution.

Tel: 0870 241 0138.

Selftrade
www.selftrade.co.uk

A £12.50 charge on all trades irrespective of the size of the trade plus the 0.5% stamp duty. Very neat, simple site that is easy to navigate. There is a demonstration dealing exercise and a 24-hour helpline. Applications can be downloaded on-line, which means you could have an account open within three days.

Tel: 01733 866399.

Share Centre
www.sharecentre.com

Deals are carried out via instructions at 9.15 a.m. 1 p.m. and 4 p.m. and your shares will be purchased at the earliest available time, subject to any price limit you set. Dealing charges are 1% of deal value, from a minimum of just £2.50 for purchases and £7.50 for sale orders. Also charges £2.50 per stock every six months. Promises that real-time dealing is on the way.

Tel: 0800 800008 or 01442 890800.

Sharepeople
www.sharepeople.com

Access to the usual FT–SE and AIM stocks but you can also trade American NASDAQ and New York Stock Exchange listed stocks too. There is a useful FT–SE 100 share price ticker on the home page providing 15-minute-delay prices.

Tel: 0870 737 8000.

StockAcademy
www.stockacademy.com

Charges £15 per trade plus a £10 fee every three months. Provides a 'walk through' trading demonstration and a news service link with financial website UK Invest.

Tel: 01223 234545.

Stocktrade
www.stocktrade.co.uk

Part of broker Brewin Dolphin. Charges 0.4% up to £3,625 with a minimum of £14.50. Customers making more than 50 deals pay the Star Trader rate of 0.2%, but the minimum charge still applies. New customers receive free company research for two months. Regular traders who make a minimum of four deals every two months keep receiving research. There is a start-up fee of £10 in advance, and an annual renewal costing the same amount. Clean site design.

Tel: 0131 240 0403.

TD Waterhouse
www.tdwaterhouse.co.uk

It's 1% commission on orders up to £1,000 and a minimum £12.95 charge. Bigger orders attract a 0.2% commission up to £45 maximum.

Tel: 0845 607 6002 or 0845 601 0403 for new accounts.

Virgin Shares
www.virgin.net

Part of the Richard Branson Virgin empire. No need to set up an account if you already have a Virgin account, in which case it's £14.50 per trade using Sharepeople's service. Look for the 'v.essentials' menu on the right-hand side of the virgin.net home page and click the stocks & shares link under the 'money' section. Has an excellent collection of links and pithy reviews of on-line brokers and share sites.

Xest
Xest.com

Part of broker Charles Stanley. Charges an initial registration fee of £20, and an annual service charge of £45. Trading fees are £14.99 per deal and orders can be placed outside trading hours to be executed as soon as the market opens. Great site, but keep an eye out for extra charges.

Tel: 0207 953 2442.

Spread Betting

As you may have gathered, this is not for the faint-hearted. Spread betting requires tungsten-reinforced brown trousers. But because it offers far greater rewards than good old-fashioned conventional investment, it is an increasingly popular way to trade on share price movements, not least because it is tax-free.

The trouble is, losses can be gut-wrenchingly large too, so for Christ's sake seriously consider using a stop loss: i.e. the mechanism which limits the amount you can lose. For more info on spread betting, how it works and who you can do it with, visit www.howtomakeyourmillion.com

Running your own website business
Why Bother

Before you rush off to stake your land claim in the virtual world, think about what you want your site to do for you, and whether you can afford the time and effort to maintain it. If you want a serious website it will certainly take a reasonable amount of your time, probably a minimum of a few hours a week. The most flexible element is the expense. Depending on how much of the work you want other people to do, it will cost as much or as little money as you want to throw at it.

If you do decide to create your own website, the first step is to register a website address. There are plenty of firms out there who'll do it for you, but your first port of call might be www.icann.com. ICANN is a non-commercial organisation which oversees the whole process and keeps track of all Internet addresses.

However, it also licenses out registration services to other companies, which will offer to perform the whole registration process for you. Normally one of these companies will charge a one-off fee to register your site name for a year, but ICANN's prices are cheap, about £30 for a year, so make sure you are not being overcharged. Many of the companies which register Internet names for you will also offer additional services, such as renewing your registration, hosting, maintaining and designing your site, and a variety of combinations in between, so make sure you have a written agreement listing exactly what you do and don't get for your money.

If a company is maintaining your site, then you send them the updates by e-mail and they will put the fresh content up on the site for you. They can also help you make sure that your site is picked up by the big Web search engines such as Yahoo!, AltaVista and Google.com.

What's in a name

Virtually every word in the dictionary has now been taken as part of the stampede for dotcom territory, but a catchy name that helps identify what the site is all about will make it more memorable and help secure repeat visits. Ideally you want it to be the phrase or word Net users would naturally think of when they are looking for information on a particular subject, though if you are creating a website for your company then it's almost certainly best to use the firm's name, and register its nicknames and variations too. Failing that, think about the name of your main product and see if that is available. If you register a really good website name, it may even be worth something.

A word of warning. In Britain it's not worth individuals adopting company names as their Web addresses, a process some-times called 'cybersquatting', since they have all been reclaimed by companies through the courts. The only get-out is if the company name is an everyday word such as egg or orange to which anyone has a legitimate claim. Don't bother trying to register those, though – egg.com was bought by the Internet bank and orange.com and all the colours went a long time before the mobile phone company got its Internet act together.

Joining the dots

Ideally you want your Web address to end in .com, such as
www.dirtybus.com. It's the most popular ending for Web addresses
and internationally recognised, so it should help generate extra
traffic. If you are looking for an audience solely in your home
country then a country-specific address ending, such as .co.uk
for Britain, will do. Ideally you will want to register both the
.com address and as many other endings as you can afford. If you
really like a particular name, but find the .com ending is already
taken, you could plump for one of a variety of other increasingly common endings such as .net. ICANN is set to release a
lot more endings by 2001, so it might be worth biding your time.

Selling the name

Wonderfully, there are firms out there who will sell your website
name to the highest bidder. This sounds great in theory but in
practice you're unlikely to receive a life-changing amount of
money for a dotcom name you came up with during one of
those tedious dinner party conversations that everyone still seems
to be having.

Give it a go, though: you've nothing to lose (except a small
commission if the sale goes through). Try www.names123.com
or www.afternic.com

Web site hosting

Unless you are Bill Gates or a computer übernerd you will have
to rent a home for your website from a company. Your site must
live on a server, one of the powerful computers that are the basic
infrastructure of the Internet. There are hundreds of companies
offering hosting, and some Web firms even give space away free,
but the basic rule is that you get what you pay for. A very basic
hosting package will cost about £100 a year, but that will rise
to about £250 for a quality package.

Choosing the right firm all gets pretty technical, but basically you will want plenty of disk space on a fast server. Ask about bandwidth, which will be a major factor determining how fast your site is to download and view. Keep an eye on the reliability – your website should be available 24 hours a day. In theory it's possible to host your website anywhere in the world, but in reality you want to host it as near to your potential audience as possible to improve speed. For a full list of firms who will host your site for you, try www.lifestyle.co.uk/ch.htm.

Site Design

Basic sites are designed using a computer language called Hyper Text Mark-up Language, or HTML for short. It's pretty simple so long as you want a simple site, and there are plenty of commercial site-building programs available, and plenty of companies and individuals for hire to do the job for you. A designer will charge about £100 to design a basic brochure site. If you want a basic e-commerce site don't expect any change from £1,000.

Image is important so have a good look around the Web and note designs you like, as well as ones you hate. Your site design should be driven by the intended audience, and the image you want to present to it. Make sure the text is large enough to read, all the features work properly, and that it is clear where each click will take the visitor. Users who fail to find what they want quickly without wading through lots of other junk will become frustrated and abandon your site. Try to divide content on to separate pages to reduce clutter, and remember – it's easier on the eye to read dark text on light backgrounds than the other way round. Flashy graphics and animation may look good, but can take ages to download on slow connections. For a full list of firms who will design your site for you, book a day off work (you'll need at least that long to type out the address) and check out www.uk computing.about.com/aboutuk/ukcomputing/cs/webdesign/

index.htm (or save time and do it yourself: there are 1,001 DIY Web design books out there).

Content

Even a simple site requiring minimal updates and content can help people know you are out there and attract new clients, so make sure address, phone and fax numbers are accurate. Ideally you will also want an e-mail function allowing people to send messages to you or your company straight from the site.

If you are a company, a basic description of the firm's product and services and terms and conditions is essential. Put your logo on the site to help build brand awareness and identity. If you want to move beyond this brochure-style site and have features such as on-line shopping and flashy graphics, then unless you're a computer expert it's almost certainly time to give the professionals a call. Keep the site up to date, and let users know when and how often it is updated. Fresh quality content will help generate regular traffic from repeat visitors, who are vital if you want to run the site on a commercial basis.

Companies that run sites which fail to deliver basic information or have dated content are shooting themselves squarely in the foot.

Financing your site

With the free offers available on the Net you can set up your own website for almost nothing. On the other hand, good sites tend to cost time and money, but there are ways you can try to recoup some of the costs, and even make some cash through advertising, sponsorship or selling goods or services on-line. To finance your site you will need to know how much it is costing, so keep an accurate note of your expenses. Secondly, you will require a plan. Financing your site successfully will not happen overnight, so you will need to make forecasts showing how and when the site will start making money. Make sure these targets are achievable, and make sure you hit them.

Advertising

To help sell advertising and gauge how much money you can generate, it helps to have basic information about the visitors looking at your site, especially the number of pages viewed on a weekly or monthly basis. A simple Web counter incorporated into the website will do that for you. Remember, advertisers will generally want to buy space on popular sites that target potential buyers of the product or service advertised, and which reflect their image.

Unfortunately the increasing number of new websites means competition for traffic grows ever more intense and there is only so much advertising to go round. That means advertising rates are cheap at about £20 per 1,000 pages viewed. If you don't want to sell ads yourself, there are people out there who will sell them for you. A useful option for small Web businesses is Valueclick at www.valueclick.com.

E-commerce

E-commerce is also highly competitive, and profit margins on most items sold on the Web are wafer-thin, so if you are going to do it make sure you get it right first time because cock-ups will generate losses. Make sure the products available are easily identifiable, reliable and that ordering is simple and orders are fulfilled swiftly. Computer hacking is less common than newspaper headlines suggest, but it can be a real pain and buyers want re-assurance, so it will help if your site is tamper-proofed.

How to make your site popular

The first step towards generating interest in your site is to let as many people know about it as possible. Don't worry if funds are short and you can't afford a celebrity-studded launch party, an army of spin doctors to make sure your launch hits the papers, or an advertising blitz – there are cheap ways of marketing your site.

First, send e-mails containing the site address to as many people as you can who might be interested, and ask them to forward it to anyone else they know who might be interested. Ask friends, family and colleagues to do the same. This so-called viral marketing is virtually cost-free, and if you are lucky it can be very effective. Basic marketing, incorporating your website address on business cards, headed paper and company vehicles, is another way to raise the site's profile. If you have a really catchy product or site it may also be worth phoning up relevant publications to interest them in your site or its story. The worst they can do is say 'no'. Use your contacts to see if they can help. Some may be willing to provide material to help beef up the site's content. Free giveaways are also a big draw, but that doesn't have to mean expensive prizes. Offering free advice is a popular way to generate traffic.

It is important to make sure that your site features on the radar screens of the Internet search engines. Register your site with as many as possible, and ensure you send them an accurate, pithy site description incorporating key words reflecting the site's content. If you are a small business it will help to generate local trade if you also include your town or city and country in the description. Try out various search engines to see whether they pick up your site.

Another option is to bring your website inside a virtual shopping mall or a website community. This works on the same principles as your local high street or shopping mall. Lots of independent retailers who might otherwise struggle to generate traffic through a stand-alone site can benefit from being under the roof of a larger, more diverse community. It is also important to develop relationships and reciprocal links with other sites, the more popular the better, so that you mutually generate traffic for one another.

Selling your data

If you collect the name and e-mail address of everyone who visits your site you can sell the data for a tidy sum: a list of just 1,000 names can net you several hundred quid. Be aware of the Data Protection Act, however: this tells you what you can and can't do and what kind of get-out clauses you should give people when asking for their details. There are several companies who will sell your data for you: go to the local library, get a copy of the *Register of Direct Marketing Services* and look in the section headed 'List managers, owners and brokers'.

I want to be a dot com millionaire

Once upon a time in the Internet world a simple on-line idea sketched on the back of a napkin was sometimes enough for investors to throw money at a project, but since the dotcom bubble has deflated it has become a whole lot harder to persuade people to help fund Internet operations. Thanks to some headline-making failures, this is especially true of e-commerce proposals, a sector in which profits have proved elusive.

That means start-up funding now is likely to come from a combination of three sources – you, your family and friends. Unless you can personally provide security such as your house (and you should take legal advice before putting up any surety) it's unlikely the bank manager will be throwing wads of dosh your way, although you may be eligible to apply for the DTI's small firms guarantee scheme, under which the DTI guarantees loans made to small firms.

However, if you have a truly outstanding idea it is still possible to attract potential investors or business angels to your cause. They will take a stake in the site in return for funding, but as an absolute minimum they will want to see a full business plan containing real-istic proposals on how your Internet company will make money.

Ideally they will also want to see an established Internet oper-ation, with lots of traffic, obvious potential and a clear forecast of when profits will arrive, as well as a management team with real business experience running an operation that already gener-ates lots of cash, and a clear idea of how and when they can sell the business on to other investors in the future at a profit.

Show me the money

If you are searching for finance or investors, a useful first port of call is specialist meetings where investors and Internet entrepre-neurs can get to meet and greet. First Tuesday, which organises meetings and seminars of budding Internet entrepreneurs, industry experts and potential investors on the first Tuesday of every month in London, is one of the better known.

Other than that, use the financial websites to identify share-holders in the smaller London-listed Internet companies and approach them for funds. These shareholders will tend to be venture capitalists, so-called private equity groups, private indi-viduals, and dedicated Internet incubator and accelerator funds. Almost all will be willing to consider a professionally presented and serious business proposal. A good place to go for advice is www.venturedome.co.uk, and the British Venture Capital Association at www.bvca.co.uk should also be able to provide some pointers.

Good luck!

PART FIVE

The Final Tally: Did I or Didn't I?

Hi there: if I were a gambler — and I very much am — I would bet heavily that you haven't actually read this book in its entirety, but have skipped to the end to see if I've made my million.

In which case, you have just learnt a valuable lesson:

To be a truly successful investor, you must realise that you will never become rich overnight. You need to be patient. There are no short cuts.

To arrive, you have to travel.

What's more, the travelling is far more rewarding than the arriving.

So go back to where you were and carry on reading!

JM

Epilogue

As Johnny Nash once sang (sort of), 'I can see clearly now the pain has gone.' It's more than six months since my experiment finally ended, and I am now, thank goodness, free from the daily mental torture that characterised most of last year. And I can now see that whole amazing Internet/stock market phenomenon for what it was.

It was, quite possibly, the most spectacular piece of self-delusion and hype ever perpetrated on the world of finance. It was, quite simply, a global frenzy, triggered by three things:

1) Greed.
2) A sudden mass awareness of the (alleged) potential of the Internet.
3) A collective rush of blood and over-exuberance caused by the dawn of the New Millenium. (If you don't believe me, check out the date when the FOOTSIE reached its all-time hight of 6,950: 31 December 1999. Since then, it's been downhill all the way.)

I got taken in, I can see that now; but I wasn't the only one. Since this book was written, countless new-economy-type firms have gone to the wall (including Adam Faith's), and many more will follow. Three trillion dollars have been wiped off the value of stock markets, worldwide. Thousands of jobs are being lost in the City: the final figure could be as high as 50,000. (One belonged to Mark, my mate who worked in the City but wasn't a wanker: he saw the way things were going and jacked it in two months ago.) Shares that were worth ten pounds just eighteen months ago are now basket cases (EG Redstone Telecom: 949p last March, 2p now). And don't think that just because you didn't get involved you're not affected: that's your pension the market is playing with.

If only. If only I'd taken notice of myself when I wondered aloud if the arrival of people like me on the scene was a sign that things were about to implode. If only I'd bet on the market going down. If only I'd realised that when I (and thousands of other small investors) were piling in through the front door the Clever Money was quietly slipping out the back. But at least I had the luck/judgement to join the exodus before the entire place burned to the ground; if I'd done my experiment this year, I would be writing this from the Bad Debts Wing at Ford Open Prison. I got out just in time. Take, for example, my biggest investment – Autonomy. I played a blinder: had I waited until now to sell, I would have lost nearly everything. Since I sold it's fallen nearly 90 per cent. (Funnily enough, Mike Lynch's problems can be traced back almost exactly to the day he reached for his Gillette G2.)

Inevitably, the recriminations are starting: those analysts I wrote about – the ones who said 'buy' while conveniently forgetting to point out that their bank stood to gain, big time, when you did – are now facing mega-lawsuits from disgruntled investors. It was a hell of a party; a lot of people now have a hell of a hangover.

Ironically, now that prices are so low, it may be a good time to pile back into the market again, but to be honest I haven't got the stomach for it any more. And I haven't got a clue when (or if) good times will return. I'm beginning to wonder, in fact, whether the whole concept of the stock market is just one big sick joke/con, and whether we wouldn't all be better off putting our money in more reliable things like banks and building societies, or buying property. The stock market may have risen non-stop for the last hundred years, but who's to say that the Good Times aren't finally over? Mind you, what do I know?

There have been pluses, though: I got a book out of it (which has sold wonderfully and, as you can see, has been published in paperback), and I can now join in a lot more conversations than I used to.

As for the website, it now feels more like a museum exhibit than a living, breathing entity. The plans to turn it into a cyber cash cow are 'on hold' (i.e. dead), but it is at least still there: when you type in the address, it suddenly pops up and peers back at you, like some cryogenically frozen oddity from another era.

And as for Sally . . . well, I never realised how interested people would be. Since this book's been published I've had several thousand e-mails: 98 per cent of which have asked, very politely, what was happening 'twixt me and her. Well . . . all will be revealed in my next book, *How to Have a Number-one Hit Single (And What to Do if You Don't)*, which, funnily enough, will be about my attempts to conquer the pop charts with my band, Surf 'n' Turf. Sorry to tease, but there really isn't enough space to go into everything that's happened right here. All I can say is . . . I never thought it would turn out like it has.

JM
Summer 2001